Music
An Understanding and Enjoyment

John Raevens
Duquesne University

KENDALL/HUNT PUBLISHING COMPANY
4050 Westmark Drive   Dubuque, Iowa 52002

Contents

Periods of Music

Vernacular Music

Opera

Music of Other Cultures

Foreword

MUSIC: An Understanding and Enjoyment is a useful, concise and fun text both for the non-music majoring college student and for anyone wanting to understand music and how it impacts their lives. People with no musical experience will learn both the varied influences upon music and as importantly the influence that music *itself* imparts—not only upon later periods and performers, but upon the larger society itself.

In a larger sense, this book could be entitled, "Music: an understanding and enjoyment of life!" Just as life encompasses politics, philosophy, art, literature, technology, religion, and interpersonal relationships, so does music. Connections between music, ideas, movements, and inventions are always there, but perhaps more discretely woven than at first glance. The use of music as a magnifying glass illustrates how and why particular political, artistic, and literary movements came about, succeeded, or even failed. Similarly, the success or failure of particular musical innovations will seem to amplify and embody its surrounding culture. Just as American patriot Patrick Henry lamented, "we shall all hang together, or we shall all hang separately," so too, shall the readers discover that music is but one of many diverse elements upon which together society hangs.

Lois J. Kalloway

Acknowledgments

Although I do not have a long list of contributors, this book would not have reached completion, if it were not for the unflagging devotion of Lois Kalloway, my wife and enthusiastic editor. Her unfailing support consoled me throughout this project. She always encouraged me to find the right word and/or appropriate expression. The pages on Rock, Women, and Jazz bear her special imprint. I owe her a special thanks for her great sacrifice. I will spend the rest of my days making it up to her.

Some other people contributed to this book's completion. Sandy Tucker reworded into more acceptable English some awkward phrases. Tom Blobner had some useful suggestions. Pearl Daube did an impeccable job typing. Without their help, the book would still be on the workbench rather than in your hands.

Music and the brain.

Some random thoughts on music's educational and healing power.

Is it true that music specifically stimulates the brain and the learning process in general? Scientists now find that the human brain is prewired for music. For instance, at the University of Toronto, Sandra Trehub is establishing that the human brain comes preloaded with music software similar to a laptop preloaded with Windows or other software.

Working with pre-schoolers, Trehub detected children discriminating pitch, tempo and melodic variations. Most surprisingly, infants smile when hearing consonant music and frown when dissonant music is being played. Is there a biological based preference in most cultures across time favoring the perfect fifths and fourths over the strident tritone?

We hear that music "has charms to soothe a savage breast"; Are those charms then essentially brain generated? Intriguingly, while we retain only small snatches of poetry or prose, such as, *We hold these truths to be self-evident...*, we can recall *scores* of tunes, even while unable to identify the composer or the title.

More controversial, is the finding that children and older adults exposed to music do better at math, as Gordon Shaw of the University of California reports, and corroborates by Frances Rauscher at the University of Wisconsin. Shaw found that children having music instruction scored 15 to 41 percent higher in ratios and fractions than their peers not having had music lessons. Musical exposure influenced only subjects requiring mathematical reasoning, leaving other academic subjects unaffected.

Josef Rauschecker of Georgetown University observed that mental music practice has a similar beneficial outcome undistinguished from actual live practice. We know that Arthur Rubenstein and Vladimir Horowitz engaged in extensive mental practicing and both were mathematically very astute.

Music's power is most astonishing among composers. No known composer, (not performer as such,) committed suicide, murder, or was clinically depressed as to interfere with their daily life. This almost defies any statistics of the general population. Is that why music is increasingly being promoted by health professionals in the healing process of chronically ill patients, especially those with Alzheimer's disease?

Introduction

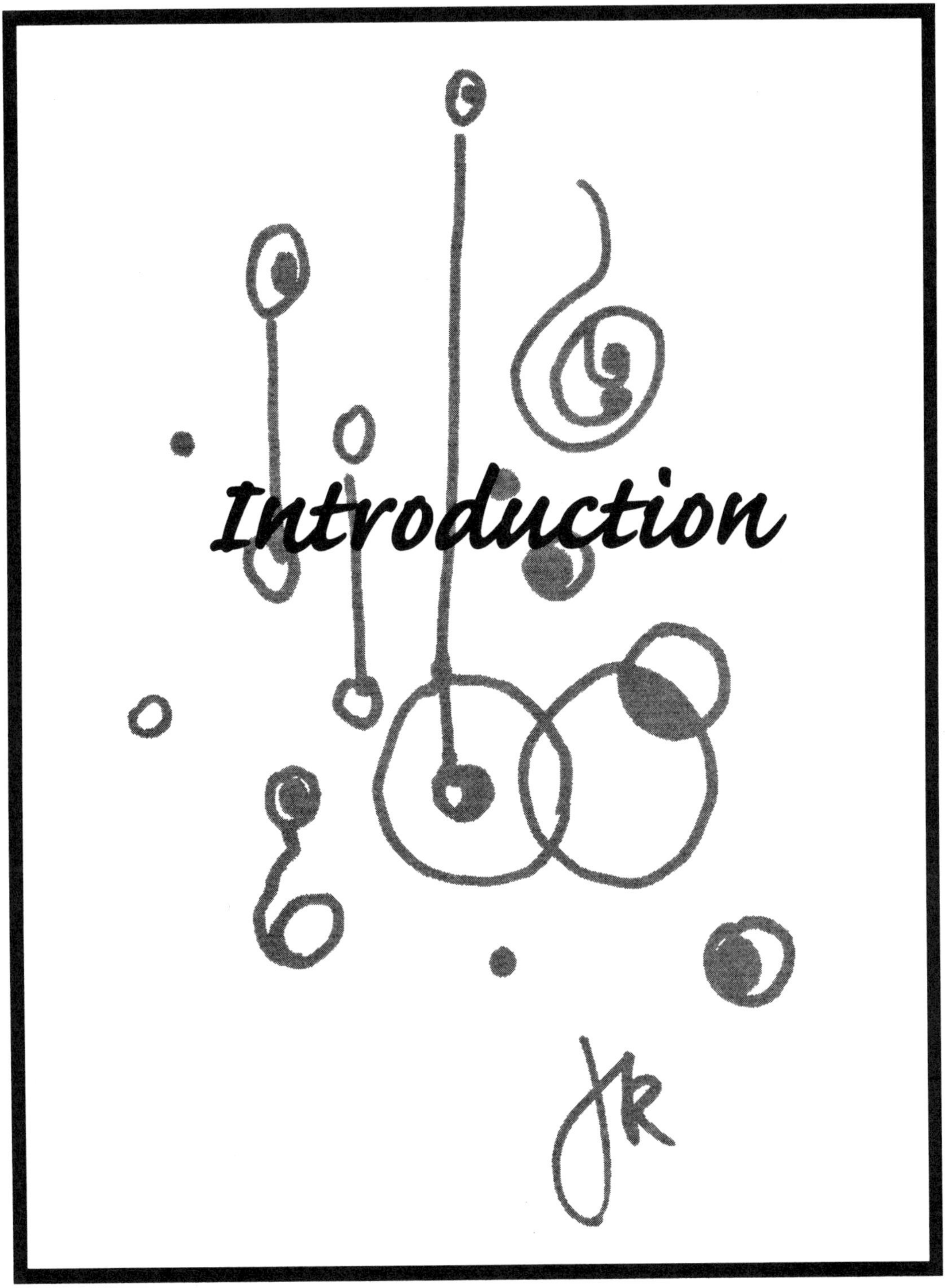

Excerpts from the National Standard of the Arts

"The Standards are one outcome of the educational reform effort generated in the 1980's, which emerged in several states and attained nationwide visibility with the publication of *A Nation at Risk* in 1983. This national wake-up call was powerfully effective. The *National Standards for Arts Education* are a statement of what every young American should know and be able to do in four art disciplines—dance, music, theatre, and the visual arts. With the passage of *Goals 2000: Educate America Act*, the national goals are written into law, naming the arts as a core, academic subject—as important to education as English, mathematics, history, civics and government, geography, science, and foreign language. In any civilization—ours included—the arts are inseparable from the very meaning of the term "education."

The arts are worth studying simply because of what they are. Their impact cannot be denied. Throughout history, all the arts have served to connect our imagination with the deepest questions of human existence: Who am I? Where am I going? Studying responses to those questions through time and across cultures—as well as acquiring the tools and knowledge to create one's own responses—is essential not only to understanding life but to living it fully.

Art education benefits the *student* as it cultivates the whole person, gradually building many kinds of literacy while developing intuition, reasoning, imagination, and dexterity into unique forms of expression and communication. An education in the arts benefits *society* because students of the arts gain powerful tools for:

1. Understanding human experiences, both past and present;
2. Learning to adapt and respect others' ways of thinking, working, and expressing themselves;
3. Understanding the influences, of the arts, for example, in their power to create and reflect cultures, in the impact of design on virtually all we use in daily life, and in the interdependence of work in the arts with the broader worlds of ideas and action;
4. Analyzing non-verbal communication and making informed judgments;
5. Communicating their thoughts and feelings in varied modes, giving them a vastly more powerful repertoire of self-expression.

Note: Italics and capital letters are mine. Italics also refer to a work's title.

Perhaps most important, the arts have intrinsic value. They are worth learning for their own sake; they provide benefits not available through any other means.

When speaking of art, we refer to the *creative works, the whole body of artworks* making up the entire cultural heritage. We also recognize that art is expressed in various ways and styles, reflecting diverse historical times and circumstances, drawing on a multitude of social and cultural resources.

Art also refers to Dance, Theatre, and the Visual arts, each encompassing varied forms and disciplines. Traditionally, we speak of seven arts: Painting, Sculpture, Architecture, Drama, Dance, Poetry, and Music. Obviously, we emphasize music, without disregarding the other arts. To read Schiller's poem *"Ode to Joy"* for example, is to experience one kind of beauty; to hear it sung by a great chorus as the majestic conclusion to Beethoven's *Ninth Symphony* is to experience beauty of an entirely different kind, an experience that for many is sublime.

Why are the arts important to us and our society? The arts have both intrinsic and instrumental value; meaning, they have worth in and of themselves. They can achieve a multitude of purposes e.g. present issues and ideas, teach or persuade, entertain, design, plan, and beautify. Lifelong participation in the arts is intrinsic for life fully lived.

Dear melodies are sweet, but those unheard are sweeter.
John Keats

Does the *Enjoyment of Music* require a text? Perhaps not. However, many students want a comprehensive book tying together all the lectures and given information. Herein is such a volume—useful for the classroom and later for reference in the endeavor of a lifelong pursuit of enjoying music. Since music is part of the arts in general, such as painting, sculpture, and architecture, as well as literature, drama, poetry and dance, these areas are also incorporated.

What is music?

Music has definitions galore—none grasping its elusive character.

Do animals make music? Are bird songs and birdcalls music? Do bird calls and other animal sounds influence composers in imitating these nature sounds?

Did Adam and Eve play music, dance, or whittle sticks?

Do we still retain the music from the ancient Greek plays. Do we know the music Nero played when entertaining the crowds at the Roman coliseum? Are the exotic Balinese exorcism rites or the Inughuit throat sons as important as Beethoven's symphonies? Is there a relation between flamenco dancing and Mozart's ballet music or the music as practiced during the Middle Ages?

After all these questions are answered, do we know what music is or its value beyond the obvious?

Bird songs are most confusing. The poets describe birdcalls as "singing." However, birds do not make music and most assuredly, not collectively. Birds neither call rehearsals nor have try-outs for song festivals, a birthday party, or just for the fun of it. Only small birds sing, and the best among them have unpretentiously colored feathers. Moreover, most birds sing by themselves, never in chorus. Only the male has a loud voice.

Surprisingly, birds do not sing in warm climates. The odd theory correlating bird songs and human music making does not stand up. In exotic countries, where folksongs are still practiced, no singing birds are found.

We still have no workable definition of what music really is. We all know what an apple is, although most perplexing to describe it to a Martian. Indeed, does music need defining? If music is something beautiful, then Keats said it best: "*A thing of beauty is a joy forever.*"

Four Elements
of Music

The most important thing in music is not in the notes!
Gustav Mahler, composer

Four Elements of Music

Rhythm; Melody; Harmony; Form

Rhythm

Rhythm is music's most primitive element. Rhythm, most broadly, is constructed of durations organized in time. Why does rhythm fascinate? Where does the pleasure arise from when we hear a rhythm? This is certainly one of the many unanswerable questions.

Rhythm is differentiated from tempo, which refers to speed. Rhythm is most important, defining music profoundly. Playing a dance too slowly is irritating; playing too fast is aggravating; worst is playing an incorrect rhythm. The adjective "rhythmic" applies to melodic or percussive patterns.

Meter is the pulse of the piece (often foot tapped). *Rhythm* subdivides those beats. It takes some knowledge to distinguish both.

Only two possibilities exist: Tic, Toc or Tic, Toc, Toc.

Different accentuation alters the feel of those patterns. For instance, <u>Tic</u> Toc versus Tic <u>Toc</u>. Similar possibilities illuminate three beat patterns. We can accent the second, third or any other combination. When individual beats are subdivided, the fun really starts!

♪ Featured Music

Prokofiev *Love for Three Oranges* Third movement, March (4/4)
Chopin *Waltzes* (3/4)
Tchaikovsky *Symphony #6* Second movement (5/4)
Dave Brubeck *Take Five* (5/4)
Stravinsky *Rite of Spring* Sacrificial dance (irregular beats)

Melody

Music's most memorable element is *melody*. A melody is often recognized without being able to place it or connect it with a specific composer. It is difficult to define a good melody, as melody writing changes with the different musical periods.

Mathematicians state that the 12 available notes create 1,302,061,344 possibilities. Obviously, not all combinations are worthwhile.

Melodies can be smooth and very singable; others are so disjointed as to be completely unmelodious.

Beethoven's *Ode to Joy* from his Ninth Symphony consists of adjacent notes, facilitating mass singing and memory. Conversely, large intervals bring tension and stress. Some pieces by Mahler, Hindemith, or Stravinsky have intervals so large prohibiting its singing and frustrating the casual listener.

A good melody consists of ascending and descending notes. Repeated notes, accented notes, or increasing note values sometimes add tension.

♪ *Featured Music*

Verdi, *La donna è mobile* from Rigoletto (very catchy melody)

Beethoven, *Ode to Joy* from the 9th Symphony (small steps)

Prokofiev, *Gavotte* from the Classical Symphony (large leaps)

Mussorgsky, *Baba Yaga* from Picture at an Exhibition (gigantic leaps)

Schoenberg, *Pierrot Lunaire* (Sprechstimme (half singing and half talking)

Harmony

The most striking musical element is *Harmony*. Different pitches sounding together produce harmony. This phenomeno, first introduced in Western music around the year 1,000 A.D., still remains largely unknown in the Eastern Hemisphere.

Harmony can be consonant (pleasing) or dissonant (harsh). Tones not belonging to a certain key are considered dissonant. Nevertheless, composers can exploit harmony's surprise value to add tension and excitement. Too many consonant chords make music dull; too many dissonances make music unsettling and disagreeable. A cooking analogy applies: too many spices make the meal unappetizing and too few makes the food flat and insipid.

Twentieth century music has become increasingly strident because of its overuse of dissonant chords.

♪ Featured Music

Palestrina, *Papae Marcellus Mass,* Kyrie (very consonant)
Stravinsky, *Rite of Spring,* dance of the Adolescents (very dissonant)
Penderecki, *Threnody* (solid masses of pitch—very strident and unsettling)

Form

Form is music's structural element, the equivalent to an architectural design. Music has two dominant features defining structure and organization: *Repeat and contrast.*

Repeat is just that, a phrasal reiteration, sometimes with a subtle variation. Redundancy is another possibility of repeating. Gregorian chant's redundancy is very great. Our own rock-and-roll music is highly based on redundancy.

Contrast brings a new melody, a new rhythm, new accompaniment, with or without a contrast in loudness, texture, or instrumentation. The possibilities are endless.

The next section is devoted completely to forms; from the smallest binary and ternary forms to larger forms, and free forms.

Forms in Music

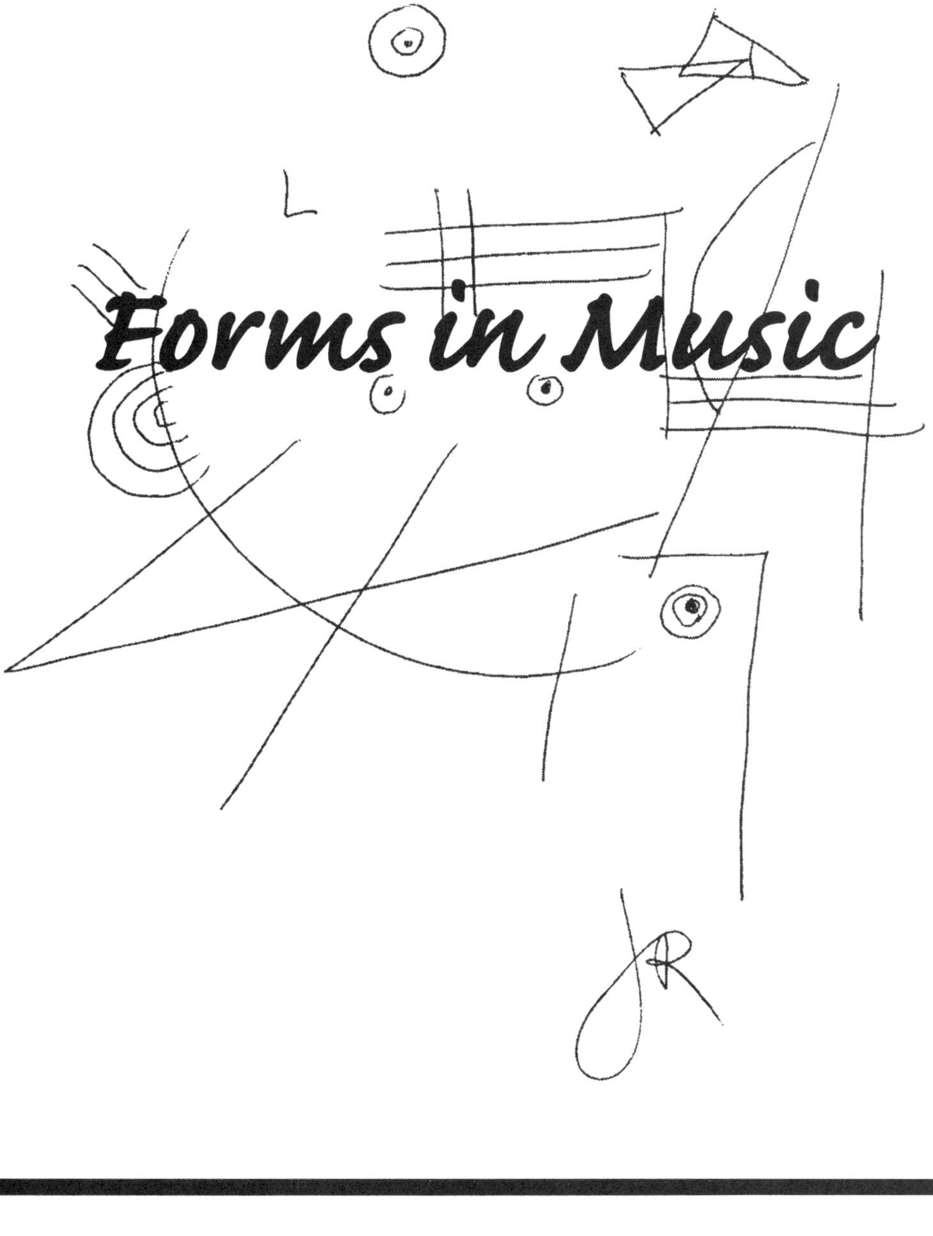

... there is music
where ever there is harmony, order or proportion;
and thus far we may
maintain the music
of the spheres.
—Sir Thomas Browne

One-Part Compositions

One-part compositions are very rare, since they lack a sense of contrast. Nevertheless, there are several pieces responding to that form. Usually the first part is repeated with some modification and/or variation. Several of Chopin's twenty-five *Preludes* are in one-part form, as are some *Preludes* of Bach's *Well tempered Clavier*.

♪ Featured Music

Frederic Chopin (1810-49), *Prelude in E minor* (1838)
Although Chopin lived all his life in Paris, his heart remained with the struggles of his Polish homeland. He never visited Poland after leaving, but remained a strong advocate, avidly studying Polish literature and culture. He died young of tuberculosis. Although he never wed, he had a tempestuous relationship with "George Sand." Chopin lived with Sand for more than ten years. The *Prelude in e minor*, one of his 25 preludes, was played at his funeral. This miniature contains wonderful music. The first part is simply repeated with some subtle, yet incisive, variations.

Béla Bartók (1881-1945), *Bear Dance* from *Ten Easy Pieces*
Hungarian by birth, he died impoverished, of leukemia, in New York City. Although a brilliant piano virtuoso, early on, he collected Eastern European folksongs—inspiring his own works. Many of his compositions, including *Bear Dance*, are for children. His own musical language is often atonal and peppered with some very sharp dissonances. With rapidly repeating bass notes and introduced by the big bass drum, the simple tune is heard sometimes in the right hand (high notes), sometimes in the left hand (low notes). It has a haunting feel.

Two-Part Compositions or Binary Form

Many compositions have two-part form. Most Lutheran-type hymns (example: *Praise to the Lord*) are in the typical AAB form, as are many Christmas carols. Listen for instance to *"Shepherds we have heard on high,"*; the second part starts with the "Gloria."

Most Baroque Period dances (1600-1750) are typically written in binary form. Bach, Handel, Telemann, and Scarlatti wrote numerous dances and sonatas in this form. These dances were often grouped together into Suites. Dances most frequently used include:

Allemande, 4/4, moderate, German

Courante, 3/2, moderate, French

Sarabande, 3/4, slow, Spanish

Minuet, 3/2, slow, French

Gavotte, 4/4, moderate, French

Bourree, 2/2, fast, French

Gigue, 6/8, quickest dance, evolved from the English/Irish jig.

Due largely to King Louis XIV, the minuet became France's premier social dance, spreading throughout Europe. Minuets were usually done in pairs. Dances in the Suites were not necessarily danced, although they could have been.

♪ *Featured Music*

J. S. Bach (1685-1750), *Orchestral Suite in D* **(Bach wrote 4 Suites for orchestra)**
Bach considered his so-called Suites as Overtures, although only their first movements are actually Overtures. As far as determined, only the first two of the Suites were written during his personally fulfilling Cothen period (1717-1723). All the dances, Bouree I and II, Gavotte, Minuet I and II are in binary form. The work concludes with a sparkling Rejouissance (Rejoicing), also in the binary form.

G. F. Handel (1685-1759), *Water Music* **(essentially a Suite of dances) (1730)**
In eighteenth century London, music was customarily performed in the parks and along the Thames river. Friedrich Bonet, a contemporary historian, tells of this music's immense popularity.

At about eight in the evening the King adjourned to his barge. Next to the King's barge was that of the musicians, about 50 in number—trumpets, horns, oboes, bassoons, German flutes, French flutes, violins, and basses ... His Majesty's approval of it was so great that he caused it to be played three times in all, twice before and once after supper, even though each performance lasted an hour. The evening was as fine as could be desired for this occasion and the number of barges and boats full of people wanting to listen was beyond counting.

What can be added to that?

G. F. Handel: *He shall feed His flock* **aria for alto and soprano, from** *The Messiah.* **(1742)** Although The Messiah was conceived as an oratorio, Handel's approach had an operatic viewpoint, with bold strokes and subjective fervor. Handel's dramatic style derives from his dynamic personality. Originally intended for alto, Mozart rewrote the second half for soprano, thereby underscoring the binary form:

He shall feed His flock like a shepherd; and He shall gather the lambs with His arm, and carry them in His bosom, and gently lead those that are with young.
Come unto Him, all ye that labor and are heavy laden, and He shall give you rest.
Take His yoke upon You, and learn of Him; and ye shall find rest unto your souls.

Isaiah xi: 11—Matt. Xi:28,29

Johannes Brahms (1833-1897), *Waltzes* **(published in 1867)**
All sixteen Brahms' Waltzes were conceived in the binary form. Brahms, a great pianist, born in Hamburg, played in taverns. In 1863 he moved to Vienna. Brahms never married, devoting his life exclusively to composition. He never indulged in the widely prevalent trend of the Program Music, music with a story-line, and perpetuated the ideals of Beethoven, whom he highly esteemed.

Igor Stravinsky (1882-1971), "I go, I go to him." *The Rake's Progress* **(1950)**
Stravinsky revived the *cabaletta*—as practiced by Mozart and later in Verdi's operas. A cabaletta is a short operatic song in a popular, simple style. Stravinsky's *The Rake's Progress*, libretto by W. H. Auden, was completed in about three years. Strikingly, Stravinsky resonates the old masters, although his signature is on every piece.

I go, I go to him.   *It will not alter*
Love cannot falter,   *Though it be shunned, etc.*
Cannot desert;   *0 should I see*
Though it be shunned   *My love in need,*
Or beforgotten,   *It shall not matter, rep*
Though it be hurt   *What he may be.*
If Love be love   *A loving heart, an ever-loving heart.*
                                                                     —W. H. Auden

Ternary Form

First introduced by the early 16th century French composers in their chansons, these showed a clearly delineated middle section, contrasting with the beginning and the conclusion. Later on, the so-called Baroque da capo arias took this procedure echoed in the instrumental music using two dances—minuet and trio. It eventually enlarged to the five-part rondo, or the scherzo with two trios. Many Christmas carols are written in the ternary form, including *Low, How a Rose is Blooming* and *0 Tannenbaum*.

The ternary form, ABA, is also used in other compositions besides the Minuet and Trio form. It perfectly corresponds to the simple proposition; in compositions we can only *repeat and contrast*. The A sections repeat, B section then interrupts, and refers back to the A section without its repetition. This form, called SONG-FORM, or in German LIEDFORM. Practically speaking, the designation ABA is clear enough. Much music is written in this simple ternary form, from second symphonic movements to larger independent compositions.

♪ Featured Music

Modest Mussorgsky (1839-1882), *Baba Yaga* from *Pictures at an Exhibition* **(1874)** Mussorgsky, member of the "Mighty Handful" was unquestionably the most original and gifted of them. The "Mighty Handful" was a group of five Russian composers: Mussorgsky; Rimsky Korsakov; Cui; Balakirev; and Borodin. Like his other friends, Mussorgsky was an "amateur," studying briefly with fellow-member Balkirev. After resigning his army commission, Mussorgsky devoted himself to composing. Born to a wealthy family who lost their estate after the emancipation of the serfs, he was plagued with nervous disorders since his teens, took to drink, and died after alcoholic epileptic attacks. When his alcoholic friend and painter, Viktor Hartmann, suddenly died, Mussorgsky wrote him a worthy tribute—a suite called *Pictures at an Exhibition*. This picture suggests to Mussorgsky *Baba Yaga*, the witch, soaring through the sky in pursuit of a new meal. It might be you!

Franz Schubert (1797-1828), *Impromptu in A flat Op. 90 #4* **(1827)**
Schubert lived his entire life in Vienna. He never held a significant position, nor won recognition during his lifetime. Yet his prodigious output included more than six hundred songs, fifteen string quartets, nine symphonies, a wealth of choral music, fourteen operas, scores of music for the theatre and voluminous piano music. He greatly admired Rossini and Beethoven. Schubert's whole life was wretched, ended mercifully by typhus. He was buried next to Beethoven as he wished. His music, reflecting his life, fluctuates between happy and sad keys. Although the music is Romantic in its expression, Schubert nevertheless stays closely connected with the traditional forms, albeit freely. This piece echoes the Minuet and Trio, although more deliberately.

G. F. Handel (1685-1759), *Water Music, Hornpipe* **(1730)**
This is Handel's most famous piece out of this dance collection. The piece itself has a royal flair, festive but dignified. Although Handel was not fond of the English, they loved his music for its pomposity and majesty, especially as it resounded over the Thames.

G. F. Handel, *I know that my Redeemer liveth* **from** *The Messiah* **(1742)**
Who does not know that perennial Christmas season oratorio, *The Messiah*? This beautiful piece moves even the most stoic listener. The middle part starts at *"and though worms"* returning to the exquisite music of *"I know that my Redeemer liveth."*

> *I know that my Redeemer liveth, and that He shall stand at the latter day upon*
>   *the earth;*
> *and though worms destroy this body, yet in my flesh shall I see God.*
> *For not is Christ risen from the dead, the first-fruits of them that sleep.*
>
> Job xix:25,26; Cor. xv:20

Classical Era Minuet and Trio Form

(as written between 1750-1800)

Minuet and trio are essentially two dances coupled together: the first one repeats itself, followed by the second dance, resulting in ABA form.

Both dances are in binary form, two part form aa/bb

The usual pattern is:
A (minuet) .... B (trio) .... A (minuet)
↓   ↓   ↓
aa/baba (binary form)   cc/dcdc (binary)   aa/ba (shortened repeat)

The large design is ABA (ternary), however, each subdivision in turn is binary.

The second dance, contrastedly, is customarily played by a smaller ensemble, hence the name Trio.

Dances were not necessarily danced, although they could have been.

Haydn probably initiated this trend of the third movement in most four movement Classical Era symphonies, being the Minuet and Trio form. The form is essentially a ternary form i.e. ABA. The middle minuet (B), played softer, called the Trio, is not necessarily scored for three players. The music of the third movement is rather amusing, in contrast to the more serious character of the first and second movements.

Typical form is AABA (Minuet), CCDC (Trio) and ABA (repeat of first Minuet)

♪ Featured Music

Franz Joseph Haydn (1732-1809), *Symphony #88* (1787)
This is a royal, pompous minuet. The Trio in contrast has a drone (bagpipe) with a country dance flavor. Haydn kept one foot in the barn, while Mozart always remained at the Court! Haydn, an Austrian, worked early on at the Hungani, a noble Esterhazy family estate, a magnificent place similar to Versailles. There he acquired an international reputation composing symphonies, masses, string quartets, and operas. After Prince Nicolaus Esterhazy died, Haydn became a freelance composer, visiting London twice.

Wolfgang Amadeus Mozart (1756-1791), *Minuet (G Minor Symphony)* **(1788)**
The first dance (A) is unusually very syncopated. The trio (B) is more pastoral and idyllic in character. Wolfgang Amadeus Mozart, as his middle name suggests, loved by God, was a divinely inspired composer. Born in Salzburg, his father took him and his sister on tour as harpsichord prodigies. Mozart was even a greater composer than his father suspected. He wrote incredibly fast; even though he died young, his output was astounding.

Wolfgang Amadeus Mozart: *Symphony #39* **K. 543**

Third movement *Menuetto — Trio — Menuetto*

0:00   Menuetto I falls into three sub-sections: a (repeated) ba' (repeated)

2:04   Trio also has its three sub-sections: c (repeated) and dc' (repeated). The music itself makes a great contrast tot he Menuetto I — c features the brand-newly invented clarinet.

3:12   Menuetto I returns. This time the first a is not repeated.

Luigi Boccherini (1743-1805), *Minuet from String Quintet in E, Op. 13.#5* **(1768)**
Bocchenini, born in Lucca, Italy, was an able cellist and a very prolific composer. He traveled to Spain, then Germany and finally returned to Madrid; dying there impoverished. He wrote voluminously, although most of his work is now forgotten. If this composition is any indication, his music was pleasing and popular.

Sergei Prokofiev (1891-1953), *Gavotte* from *The Classical Symphony* **(1916-18)**
Patterned after the Classical Minuet and Trio form, this gavotte adheres to the original "classical" form, though heavily trimmed and shortened. Prokofiev studied under Rimsky-Korsakov. He lived abroad from 1918-1927. When he returned to the Soviet Union he was forced by the government to write in a more accessible idiom, "simple tunes for simple people" as the prescription read. It is almost impossible to know if he conformed willingly or by decree. Nonetheless, this *Sixth Symphony* and some other works were officially condemned in 1948. As a final irony, he died the same day as Stalin!

Maurice Ravel (1875 - 1937), *Rigaudon* from *Tombeau de Couperin.* **(1914-17)**
This Suite has the typical Ravel sound within a traditional form. Ravel, a French composer, became an exponent of the then-prevailing Impressionism. He was a

brilliant orchestrator, although curiously, most of his work (including this composition) was conceived for the piano and only later orchestrated. He was a meticulous chiseler and his output was relatively small, although always of the highest quality.

Scherzo and Trio

Beethoven apparently introduced this much faster and less dance-like movement into the symphony. Based on the minuet and trio form, the scherzo was no longer an amusing intermezzo, or a curtsey dance, but a full-fledged entity with an entirely different intent. By the Romantic Period (1830-1910) the scherzo had its own independent life with Chopin, Schubert and others writing many independent scherzi.

♪ Featured Music

Beethoven, (1770-1827), *Symphony #5, third movement*
While keeping the basic form of the minuet and trio, this piece starts very mysteriously. Soon a four-note theme hammers—recalling of the first theme of the first movement. The trio section, a fierce chase between voices, finally merges into the greatly changed and subdued scherzo. Beethoven then miraculously, after an evasive cadence, couples that movement onto the final movement without its traditional separation. This metamorphic passage is like a Phoenix rising from the ashes into the sunburst of the first theme of the last movement.

Peter Tchaikovsky, (1840-1893), *Symphony #4, Scherzo* (1877)
This scherzo starts out with a pizzicato for all the strings, sounding like a giant ensemble tamburitza, Russia's beloved instrument. The trio, incorporating a march-like section, soon returns to the pizzicato scherzo of the beginning. Tchaikovsky, born near St. Petersburg, was the aristocrat of the Russian style. He kept aloof from the more overt nationalism of the "Mighty Five." The symphony was dedicated to "my best friend" Madame Nadezhda von Meck, his wealthy patron. His music is both melancholic and sad. Most of his music was written for ballet, and this scherzo also could be used as ballet music.

Johannes Brahms (1833-1897), *Symphony #2 third movement* (1877)
As a distinctive feature, Brahms employs two trios. Brahms, born in Hamburg, Germany, moved at age thirty to Vienna. He is generally considered Beethoven's

epigone disciple of Beethoven, although his music is generally gentler and less dramatic than his mentor.

Dimitry Shostakovich (1906-1975), *Allegretto from The Symphony #5* **(1937)**
Shostakovich, the very gifted Russian composer, was repeatedly reprimanded by the Soviet government for writing unmelodious, harsh-sounding music, so needed a work that would return him to good graces. For the twentieth anniversary of the Russian Revolution he presented his *Fifth Symphony,* as a "creative response to just criticism." The thunderous applause surely was rewarding to him—assuring his triumphant return to the fold. After the stem first movement, the scherzo of the second movement gave a welcome relief. After a hesitant cello and basses opening, a rather pleasant and engaging tune lightens the atmosphere. This Symphony has lasting qualities.

Paul Hindemith (1895-1963), *Turandot* from *Symphonic Metamorphosis* **(1945)**
Hindemith, born in Frankfurt, Germany was a prominent teacher, performer, composer and public figure in demand throughout his life. Besides that, he was most instrumental in changing 20th century music. The variations on a theme of Weber's Turandot Overture drives relentlessly, interrupted only by a jazz-influenced trio. Because of his musical radicalism, he was ordered to leave his country. Moving first to Turkey in 1933, he finally settled in New England, teaching at Yale University. Nostalgia drove him back to Europe after World War II.

Rondo Form

The Rondo form is based on the periodic return of the initial theme. There are two types:

1. Baroque Ritornello
2. Classical Era Rondo form

The Baroque Ritornello

This form originated in poetry. The French Rondeau was especially cherished during the Baroque Period. The initial theme, the ritornello, returns in its entirety or in fragments again and again. The intervening sections are called episodes. The first rondeaus were an important form of medieval French music, played frequently by 13th century trouveres. The recurring refrain periodically interrupts the story carried along with numerous couplets. The madrigals of the 14th and 15th centuries retain this form virtually intact. The Rondeau form is still used in contemporary ballads (example: *You Light Up My Life*).

♪ Featured Music

Louis Daquin, (1694-1772), *Noel in G major* (1732)
Most popular Christmas organ music is based on the Rondeau principle with elaborate variations of the refrain. Daquin lived and died in Paris. As a very young boy he played for Louis XIV. By the age of twelve, he replaced the organist at the famous Sainte-Chapelle, later becoming organist of the Royal Chapel in 1739, where he remained until his death. His playing has a remarkable, unfaltering precision.

J. S. Bach (1685 - 1750), *Brandenburg Concerto #2, first movement* (1721)
Johann Sebastian Bach was born into a family of musicians at Eisenach, a small town in Thuringen, Germany. A lengthy dedication, in awkward French, bequeathes these concertos to Duke Christian-Ludwig, Margrave of Brandenburg, humbly reminding his Highness of the "little talents" God has given him. Was Bach trying to solicit the Margrave for a job? Why then were these concerti never opened by the latter? All six concerti have the same type of rondo form, with small ensembles playing against the tuttis of the ritornello, as cultivated by Vivaldi.

Antonio Vivaldi (1678- 1741), *"La primavera"* from *Four Seasons* (1725)
Vivaldi was born in Venice, and died under somewhat obscure circumstances in Vienna. He was a priest, nicknamed "il prete rosso," perhaps because of his red hair. As chaplain of a home for orphaned girls, he required them to study music under his tutelage. Of his more than 250 concerti, his *Four Seasons* remain a perennial favorite. Between the returning ritornellos, he depicts little scenes. The first movement featured a bird concert, a flowing stream, and a thunderstorm before returning soon to a bird concert. Program music was still rare, and most of his music has titles suggesting picturesque scenes and tone-painting. The haunting question of why he went to Vienna remains unanswered.

The Classical Era Rondo Form

The Classical Era Rondos are generally charming and pleasing. They are mostly placed as the last movement in symphonies, quartets or piano sonatas. The overall form is usually ABACA. The A's are called refrains, and the other interjections are commonly referred to as episodes. Very often a coda is added (coda is the name for "tail piece").

♪ Featured Music

Franz Joseph Haydn (1732 - 1809), *Trumpet concerto in E flat major* **(1796)**
Basically this is an optimistic piece, displaying an amazing free flow of dazzling virtuoso trumpet playing. It is written in a typical rondo-form with a slightly larger development in the middle. It may be outlined as ABABA-C-AB-coda. The refrain A is a high-spirited tune well-suited for the trumpet. Theme B is just as playful. Towards the end is a sudden pause, even a hint of a cadenza, one of the many witty surprises in Haydn's compositions.

Ludwig von Beethoven (1770-1827), *Bagatelle "Für Elise"* **(1810)**
This is undoubtedly Beethoven's best known piano piece, clearly written for an unknown young lady. Scholars believe that the inscription was really "Für Therese," perhaps misreading the original, as Therese Malfatti had been one of Beethoven's many acquaintances. The lighthearted refrain is frequently interrupted by agitated passages.

W. A. Mozart (1756-1791), *Eine kleine Nachtmusik* **(Summer 1787)**
A charming serenade for strings only. It is unknown what prompted Mozart to write these masterly crafted jewels. While the second and last movements are in the conventional rondo form, he poured only divine music into it.

Felix Mendelssohn (1809-49), *Wedding March* **from** *Midsummer Nights Dream*
Mendelssohn finished this work on August 6, 1826. He was seventeen! This remains one of the most beloved wedding marches. Mendelssohn, grandson of the Jewish philosopher Moses Mendelssohn, was raised a Lutheran. Besides being a very prolific composer, he started a successful Bach revival in 1829. His music combines Romantic glow within Classical form.

Franz Joseph Haydn (1732-1809), *Trumpet Concerto in E flat Major* **(1796)**
Written for a Vienna court trumpeter who invented a keyed trumpet capable of playing a complete chromatic scale. It was the forerunner of the valve trumpet invented circa 1840.

Third Movement

Allegro

Rondo form with added development section as was customary in the Classical period.

0:00   Refrain theme in the violins, with its repeat in full orchestra
0:38   Refrain theme in trumpet, also repeated
1: 07   Verse I in trumpet with some virtuoso passages, trills and fanfares.
1:46   Refrain theme returns in trumpet, replied by the orchestra
2:04   Verse II in trumpet with acrain some virtuoso passages
2:36   Refrain theme ushered in by the trumpet with an orchestra reply.
2:54   Verse III (development-like passage) with even more demanding trumpet passage.
3:27   Coda. Trumpet vanes the refrain theme with trills, repeated notes, octave leaps and fast runs giving it a full display of its capabilities.

One last refrain theme return and a few closing chords concludes Haydn's most popular piece.

Charles Ives (1874-1954), *The Unanswered Question* **(1906)**

This composition is extremely interesting, especially considering that it was written circa 1906. It consists of three independent bodies of sound. The background strings hardly move, (the cosmos?) a muted offstage trumpet asks seven questions (refrain) and four flutes answer. Only the answers (episodes) change and become increasingly louder, faster, and angrier. The last question remains unanswered, while the strings play on undisturbedly. Charles Ives was born in Danbury, Connecticut. Although an insurance broker by trade, he still wrote five symphonies, numerous songs, several choral works, and some piano sonatas. A true pioneer, all his work written before 1920 uses later devices e.g. *Polytonality, Poly-rhythms, quarter-tones* and other novelties. He was ignored until 1939, but in 1946 Leonard Bernstein discovered and eventually conducted his *Symphony #3* at Carnegie Hall in New York City. Schoenberg proclaimed Ives a "great composer."

George Gershwin (1898-1937), *It's Wonderful* **(1930)**
Gershwin unquestionably is one of America's most gifted composers. His language, unabashedly jazz, uses the "classical" forms to hold everything in place. He was born in Brooklyn, New York, of poor Jewish immigrants. His folks having no musical instrument meant not until his teens was his musicality awakened. He soon became a piano-pounder at a shop in "Tin Pan Alley" and realized that he too could write popular tunes. The song Swanee, published around 1919, sold millions of copies, and established him as a reputable song writer. In 1924 he wrote his masterpiece Rhapsody in Blue, a jazz piano concerto that made him famous. In 1935 he wrote his only opera Porgy and Bess, moving to Hollywood shortly after its production to write film music. An inoperable brain tumor took him to an early death.

Theme and Variations

There are two basic two types of variations, *Sectional* and *Continuous.*

Sectional Variations

The *Sectional* variations use most often well-known tunes. The variations retain the same overall structure of the tune (theme) with typically a short break between the different variations. The theme itself is transformed either melodically, harmonically and/or rhythmically with even the tempo possibly differing amongst the variations. Besides these technical interventions, the theme is thereby transfigured—changed not only musically but also emotionally. This is one of the older forms and was used since the early 17th century by such Elizabethan virginalists in England (players of an English harpsichord) as Byrd and Tallis, and elsewhere, Sweelick in Holland and Buxtehude in Germany.

♪ Featured Music

Sweelinck, *Six Variations on "My Young Life is Ending"* **(early 1600)**
Jan Pleterszoon Sweelinck is the last of the great composers from the Netherlands. A musical heir of the English Virginal School, he became a sought after teacher to many German composers. This simple folk tune is literally lifted into the sphere of great art through Sweelinck's distinguished craftsmanship.

Sweelinck's importance lies in his virtuoso-like exploitation of the technical possibilities of the harpsichord or organ, rapid passages, scales, etc. His contribution influenced scores of composers including Bach and Handel.

Mozart (1756-1791), *Twelve Variations on "Ah! Vous direz-je, maman "* **(Summer 1778)** Is anything musically impossible for Mozart? This innocent little tune, known as *Twinkle, Twinkle, Little Star,* becomes a big star under Mozart's metamorphic transformation.

Beethoven (1770-1827), *Seven Variations on "God save the King"* **(1804)**
A simple tune becomes an event. Initially, Beethoven retains the anthem's plainness, but gradually the tune, under the sweep of figurations and bravura, is lifted into the realm of an extensive fullscale piano piece. Only Beethoven can alter its appearance and change it into a march, a scherzo and eventually a brilliant finale.

Cesar Franck (1822-90), *Symphonic Variations* **(1885)**
Franck was the most German of all French composers, his models being Bach, Beethoven, Liszt, and Wagner. Born in Liège, Belgium, by age twenty-two he settled in Paris where he played the organ for thirty-two years at St. Clothilde, a very prominent Parisian church. This quasi piano concerto wonderfully intersperses variations on two original themes. This composition is full of warmth and genuine human feeling.

Charles Ives (1872-1954), *Variations on "America"* **(1891)**
At age seventeen Charles wrote these variations for his church's Fourth of July celebration. Originally written for organ, it sounded brand new when William Schumann, head of the Julliard School of Music, orchestrated it in the late nineteen-fifties. The variations are a kaleidoscopic portrait of American society; diverse, bold, optimistic, colorful, and urban. With its high school band, Spanish rhythms, English country dances, and jazzy rhythms, it defines American life more than words ever did.

George Gershwin (1898-1937), *Variations on "I Got Rhythm "* **(1934)**
This song illustrates Gershwin's genius. Musically insecure, he asked many composers for composition lessons. He unsuccessfully solicited Stravinsky, Schoenberg and Ravel. Schoenberg simply told him, "I would only make you a bad Schoenberg, and you're such a good Gershwin already!" What Gershwin lacked in craftsmanship he amply made up with pure musicianship. The syncopation creates a very jazzy experience. Was the *Rhapsody on a Theme of Paganini* by Rachmaninov, of the same year, his model? There is reason to believe so, since both artists use the piano as the main vehicle.

Continuous Variation

The Continuous Variation is known variously as Passacaglia, Chaconne, Ground, etc. It is based upon a slow, continuously repeating bass, while the upper voices make variations overhead.

The Continuous Variation is a typical Baroque form, already used by Byrd (1543-1623), the English Virginalists, and in Monteverdi's 1607 opera, *Orfeo*.

♪ Featured Music

Johann Sebastian Bach (1686-1750), *Passacaglia and Fugue for Organ* **(1717)**
This monumental work contains twenty variations. This piece alone would have insured Bach's musical immortality. The first nine variations build up to a climax, then the theme moves exceptionally to the upper voice for a few variations. Variation thirteen and fourteen lessen the tension, only rebuilding it to a tremendous climax. The twentieth variation merges into an engaging fugue, while the passacaglia theme artfully interweaves into it twelve times.

Johann Pachelbel (1653-1706), *Canon In D major* **(1699)**
Pachelbel's "canon" is frequently used in films and commercials. Constructed conventionally, it has a repeating bass and two upper voices imitating in canonic fashion—hence its name. Pachelbel was long-time organist at the St. Sebaldus church in Nurnberg, Germany. He taught Bach's brother, who in turn instructed Johann Sebastian, thus making him Bach's spiritual ancestor.

Note: A canon is similar to *Three Blind Mice* sung with different partners, starting at different times.

Johann Pachelbel, *Canon in d*

28 canonic variations set over a passacaglia bass, repeating 28 times as well.

Originally written for three solo violins, bass and harpsichord.

Note: Canon is a form similar to *Row, row your boat* and passacaglia is a repeating bass, in this case of 8 slow moving notes. This piece is often used for processions.

Henry Purcell (1659-95), *Dido's Lament from Dido and Aeneas* **(1689)**
Purcell, a life-long London resident, was truly England's glory. At age twenty he became Westminster Abbey's organist and at twenty-three the Royal Chapel organist. Unfortunately, he died rather young, victim of a cold resulting from being kept waiting for admittance to his house. He was buried beneath Westminster Abbey's organ. The obituary inscription reads: "gone to that Blessed Place Where only his Harmony can be exceeded." *Dido and Aeneas*, and particularly this aria, quoted below, is truly a Baroque masterpiece. Dido's melody moves over a repeated bass, occasionally making dissonants with it. The chromatic descending bass line movingly expresses Dido's tragic fate. Dido and Aeneas's story comes from the writings of Virgil (70 B.C.-19 B.C.). Aeneas (having lost his country, Troy) is ordered by the gods to seek a new empire. One day he lands in Carthage and falls in love with its Queen, Dido. But the gods tell him to move on to find his own country, as this was not his, but Dido's place. When he leaves, Dido feeling betrayed and heartbroken, in despair kills herself.

Recitative	*Thy hand, Belinda! Darkness shades me.*
	On thy bosom let me rest.
	More I would, but death invades me.
	Death is now a welcome guest.
Aria	*When I am laid in earth,*
	May my wrongs create no trouble in thy breast
	Remember me, but ah! Forget my fate.
	—Virgil (30 B.C.)

Maurice Ravel (1875-1937), *Passacaille from The Piano Trio* **(1914)**
This is the third movement of a most intriguing set of pieces for piano, violin and cello, closing Ravel's pre-war production. The slow moving, triple-time bass line is somewhat unique for its genre, but as usual, Ravel manipulates it creatively. The theme itself also undergoes variation and rearrangement as the piece progresses. The fifth variation is the climax of the piece, then the piece gradually recedes in volume, while increasingly compressing the theme. The imminent war left Ravel bitter and depressed over the loss of many friends; Ravel's resulting illness, and the disappointing military experience, which impaired his creative output. Many years passed before he could resume his art.

Basso Ostinato

While not strictly within the variation technique, the *Basso ostinato* uses a similar device employing an *obstinate bass*, (basso ostinato) usually of three to five notes. Unlike the passacaglia, the theme is short and much faster, and can repeat as much as a hundred times! It has the unique ability to bring excitement and tension within the piece.

♪ Featured Music

George Bizet (1838-75), *Carillon* **from** *L'Arlesienne, Suite No. 1* **(1872)**
The overall design of the piece is ABA. The A sections employ the "basso ostinato" using the bright pealing of the Carillon (church bells). The B section momentarily interrupts the festive atmosphere with a quieter interlude. Gradually the bells are reintroduced, resuming their festive clamor. The bells, pealing more than an hundred times in the piece, express the celebration of a beautiful feastday. It takes the genius of a Bizet to create out of these many repetitions a magnetic, exalting piece.

Bizet was a very gifted French composer who died at age thirty-six from throat cancer, which was aggravated by his beloved *Carmen* opera being cruelly rejected at its premiere. Now this opera has become one of the most performed productions of all time. His career started very young; he entered the Paris Conservatory just before his tenth year! At seventeen he wrote his only symphony, a very mature work, still favored among music lovers.

Alexander Borodin (1833-87), *Polovetzian Dances* **from** *Prince Igor* **(1869)**
Borodin, illegitimate son of a prince, was one of the "Mighty Five," a Russian group of composers. Borodin, being a chemistry professor, was never a full-time composer, so many of his compositions remain unfinished. This piece is typically Russian; wild, unbridled, obstinate, and visceral. The "basso ostinato," four descending notes in the bass, drives the dance into a frenzy ending in a burst of magnificent sounds. While the opera Prince Igor failed, the music survived.

Igor Stravinsky (1882-1971), *Part III* **from the** *Symphony of Psalms* **(1930)**
After the savage *Rite of Spring*, Stravinsky suddenly changed course, with the *Pulcinella* ballet Suite marking a new evolution within his composing style. It became known as the "neo-classic" style.

This symphony, commissioned to commemorate the fiftieth anniversary of the Boston Symphony Orchestra, with the proviso that he would write something "popular." This is one of the twentieth century's undisputed masterpieces. He chose the Psalms as basis for the entire work and Psalm 150 for the last movement. It is a psalm of exaltation with David dancing before the Ark.

This movement falls into three distinct sections, beginning with a slow introduction praising God in His Sanctuary. The rapid passage, inspired by the vision of Elijah's chariot climbing the Heavens, as Stravinsky himself indicates. When the music finally slows at "laudate eum in tympano et choro" (praise Him with the timbrel and dance) the bass instruments start the basso ostinato. Eventually, at "Laudate eum in cymbalis" (praise Him upon the loud cymbals), a four note figure in the bass is repeated very deliberately about thirty times. It sounds as if hewn in granite. The orchestration is stark, mostly brass, some woodwinds, but no violins; the all male chorus, including a boys' choir, give it a Byzantine flavor.

Sonata-Allegro Form

The Sonata-Allegro form first developed during the Classical Era. Its beginnings are rooted in the Pre-Classical period. It is the only form with *two themes*. The main divisions are: *Exposition, Development, and Reexposition.* The Sonata-Allegro form is similar to an Opera. The *Exposition,* with its twin themes, represents the two main characters. The *first theme* is usually strong, rhythmic, and assertive—the masculine element. The *second theme* is softer, more melodious, and subdued—the feminine element. Between the two different keys of the themes a transition is inserted. The latter passage is fragmented, non-thematic, and harmonically unstable. The great contrast between the themes creates great potential for conflict in the development. Up to and including the early Beethoven, the *exposition* was repeated. It re-enforced recall of the themes. The *development's* building material are the two themes (rarely a third theme) making it a highly dramatic section. The *recapitulation* returns with the themes back into their original order, but this time both in the same home key. Most often the composer adds a lengthy coda.

The Sonata-Allegro form became the keystone of the Classical period. Thus the sonata form was used for piano, solos with piano, trios, quartets, quintets, symphonies and almost all music written in the Classical Period. Because of its strong design, the Sonata-Allegro form survived the Romantic period, and even the twentieth century still occasionally uses it.

The Sonata-Allegro form is always the first movement of any Symphony, Piano Sonata, and any chamber work of the Classical Period. Eventually, it was also used for the last movement, increasingly replacing the customary Rondo.

♪ Featured Music

W. A. Mozart (1756-1791), *Overture* **to** *The Marriage of Figaro,* **(1786)**
The Overture, in the Sonata-Allegro form, without a development, remains eternally electrifying and energetic, and a faithful reflection of Mozart's most successful opera. The two themes resemble two different personalities. The first theme is assertive, strong and dramatic, while the second theme contrasts entirely, with its delicate and pleasing disposition. If any one opera established Mozart as the master of this genre this was it. The opera has always enjoyed a huge success , even to this day. Mozart greatest desire was to be an opera composer; he only wrote some piano concertos, and occasional symphonies out of necessity or for his friends.

One question remains: Was Mozart hurrying to finish the Overture and simply skipped the development? Or was it so designed all along?

Wolfgang Amadeus Mozart: *The Marriage of Figaro* **Overture (1786)**

Sonata-allegro form without a development section

0:00	1st theme, strong, assertive and energetic—immediately repeated
0:46	transition to the
1:26	2nd theme—gentle and in contrasting melodious style
1:50	recapitulation—1st theme not repeated
2:19	2nd theme and repeated
3:11	Coda—starting from very soft to a climactic ending.

Mozart, *G minor Symphony fourth movement* **(1788)**
The symphony begins with a curious introductory "vamp" (a simple accompaniment, improvised for the occasion) that both starts the motor and sets the tone. The theme, in complete symmetry, nevertheless strikes a mood of tension and uneasiness. The second theme is relaxed, easy and simple, a complete contrast from before. The development contains some of Mozart's strongest utterances.

Why did Mozart write this symphony, together with two other ones and within six weeks, at incredible speed? He even revised the score, adding two clarinets and rewriting the oboe part to compliment them. Was a benefactor waiting in the wings? It appears that he may never have heard a live performance of these symphonies. Although Mozart was at the height of his powers, his income was modest. We may perhaps never know what went wrong with some planned public concerts.

Ludwig van Beethoven (1770-1827), *Symphony #5, first movement* **(1808)**
Beethoven, although born in Bonn, Germany, lived practically all his life in Vienna, Austria. His initial fame was both as a pianist and improviser of great power and originality. Initially Beethoven listened to and absorbed the prevailing masters. After his third symphony, Beethoven's musical language extended beyond the structural length and expressive communication of all his contemporaries. His *Fifth Symphony* belongs to his so-called "heroic period," wherein he finds his own mature voice. With this most famous theme, Beethoven creates a highly personal expression, a theme permeating the entire symphony. He is at his best. The thundering, strong first theme contrasts with the gentler second theme, even though it was siphoned from the first motive. The development becomes the battlefield of conflicting forces—a clash between darkness and despair (minor key). In the end, the minor key is victorious, even though the major key was instrumental for its success. Particularly notable is the repetition of the first theme in the reexposition, where a single oboe is the sole survivor albeit behaving as a sleepwalker in the night. The coda resembles a second development, full of vigor while trying to postpone the inevitable ending. In technique and form Beethoven is a Classicist, but his expressive scope leans toward the Romantic Era.

Peter Tchaikovsky (1840-1893), *Romeo and Juliet, Overture-fantasy* **(1869)**
At age ten, Tchaikovsky moved to St. Petersburg, Russia where he first studied law but soon realized that he was not "a clerk but a musician." His *Romeo and Juliet* is one of his early successes.

After a lengthy, hymn-like introduction, (the monks praying), the first theme enters forcefully, sounding belligerent with its clanging cymbals (fighting theme), while the second theme (love theme) is highly emotional, luscious and memorable—a perfect model of contrasting themes. Tchaikovsky makes the most of the conflict in the development. The Coda is a funeral march, ending remarkable on a curious upbeat tone. Tchaikovsky's music, with its inherent Russian strain, strong Italian sensuousness, and built with Germanic structural sense, has become indispensable to the musical world.

Ludwig von Beethoven: *Symphony NO. 5 in C minor,* op.67 (1808)

First movement: allegro con brio

Sonata-allegro form

Exposition

0:00   First theme, immediately repeated a step lower.
0:08   first theme developed in strings merged into a transition to the second theme
0:46   solo French horns (horn-call) introduce Second Theme
1:28   Exposition is repeated from the beginning

Development

2:57   Mostly first theme
3:33   Horn-call prominently used in upper-strings
3:34   woodwinds in dialogue with lower strings, great decrescendo
4:05   Horn-call motive breaks through twice leading into the

Recapitulation

4:18   First theme with full orchestra
4:38   Suddenly Beethoven seems lost and retains only a oboe solo
4:50   transition leading to
5:12   second theme, introduced by the now familiar horn-call
Coda
5:54   Beethoven still going strong, not giving in to its expected end
6:29   new material in strings, answered in powerful dialogue with lower strings.
7:05   First theme in full force and repeated a step lower.
       Suddenly very soft, followed by some powerful concluding chords.

Peter Ilyich Tchaikovsky: *Russian dance* from his *"The Nutcracker"* **Suite.**

Perhaps the shortest piece Tchaikovsky ever wrote, although it is part of his charming Christmas party for children.

The piece is typically Russian, fast and full of vitality and fire. It has an irresistible feel of "get up and go." His "Nutcracker contains some of his most spontaneous and enchanting music. No one ever get's tired of hearing it year after year.

Sergei Prokofiev (1891-1953), *Classical Symphony, first and last movement* **(1917)** This is a short, witty imitation of the "old" form, but with new wine! Besides being a virtuoso and recitalist, Prokofiev had comparable composing talent.

Béla Bartók (1881-1945), *Concerto for Orchestra, first movement* **(1943)**
The first movement of the "Concerto" is a rather stem and intense showpiece for an orchestra of virtuosos. The long, brooding introduction evolves into a fast, vigorous first theme. The second theme is softer, delicate, and folk-like, especially following a blast of granite-like trombones. The development is short and pointed. In the recapitulation the themes appear in reverse order. The previously heard trombone theme gives the movement an assertive ending.

Sergei Prokofiev *"Classical Symphony "* **(1917) Third movement:** *Gavotte—Trio—Gavotte*

Fashioned after Mozart's model but greatly shortened. A spoof and satire. The whole piece lasts only 1:31.

0:00   The initial melody is bold, with large leaps—the repeat almost feels like its inverse.

0:40   Trio is more regular and with prescribed repeats. The melodies are anchored on a bagpipe-like drone.

1:06   Gavotte I returns but just a bit slower and more pompous. It all ends like a vapor.

Program Music

Tone painting was always a preoccupation of composers. High, low, soft, and loud can be used to evoke emotions, scenes, and circumstances. Long notes were assigned to sleep, rests to death, rapid passages to exaltation, chromatic passages to sorrow and grief, and trumpets to usually kingly music. Music can imitate galloping horses, thunder and lightening, bird songs, church bells and sirens, and many other phenomenon that we would readily recognize. Tonepainting can also evoke moods including joy, depression, sadness, jubilation and many other shades of emotion. Countless compositions have a programmatic content. Examples include: Hector Berlioz: *Symphonie Fantastique*, Tchaikovsky: *1812 Overture*, Bedrich Smetana: *Ma Vlast*, Paul Dukas: *The Sorcerer's Apprentice*, Richard Strauss: *Till Eulenspiegel*, Beethoven: *Symphony #6, The Pastorale*, Ferde Grofe: *Grand Canyon Suite* and many, many more.

♪ Featured Music

Franz Schubert (1797-1828), *Erlkönig, Ballad for Voice and Piano* (1815)
Schubert lived only in Vienna. Contemporary with Beethoven, whom he kept in very high esteem, Schubert was unquestionably the grand master of the German lied. He wrote 600 songs for voice, six Latin masses, several operas and nine symphonies. Although a very prolific composer, he never had an official position nor gained any recognition during his lifetime.

The Goethe text displays the sort of supernatural content favored by nineteenth-century composers. The text presents four characters, each having a specific role. The narrator sings in a matter-of-fact tone, the father tries to calm the child, the child is scared and the Angel of Death sounds alluringly enticing. The galloping figure played by the piano represents the horses hurrying through the night. At the very end, when they finally arrive home, the horses stop, and the father looks with disbelief at his dead child.

Who is riding so late through the night and the wind?

Piano introduction, rapid Repeated notes and motive in the bass.

It is the father with his child;

he holds the child close in his arms, holding him close and securely.

My son, why do you hide your face so anxiously?	voice in low register
Father, don't you seethe Erlking? The erlking with his crown and train?	voice in high register
My son, it is a streak of mist?	low register
Dear child, come, and go with me! I'll place nice games with you. Many beautiful flowers grow along the shore; My mother has many golden garments.	cajoling; high register
My father, don't you hear the Erlking whispering promises to me?	
Be quiet, be still, my child; the wind is rustling the dead leaves.	
My handsome boy, will you come with me? My girls are waiting for you; they are starting the dance every night, and will cradle, dance and sing you to sleep.	playful; alluring
My father, don't you see the Erlking's daughters In the shadow?	outcry
My son, I see it clearly The old trees look so dark.	reassuring
I love you, your handsome figure delights me! If you are not willing, I may have to force you!	enticing and threatening
My father, he is taking hold of me! The Erlking is hurting me!	scared
The father shakes, but rides on; he holds the groaning child in his arms, he reaches the house weary and exhausted:	piano suddenly stops
in his arms the child was dead.	

Franz Liszt (1811-1886), *Totentanz* (*Dance of Death*) (1853)
The Totentanz consists of variations on the Dies Irae, a chant heard during the Catholic funeral mass. The programatic content is based on a painting of the Black Death of the mid-fourteenth century. In some ways, the piece is a piano concerto, as that instrument features most prominently. The musical content becomes increasingly oppressive and horrifying, expressing the terrifying consequences of the plague.

Liszt was the prodigy pianist of his time. He never married, yet he had countless affairs and even sired a daughter, Cosima, who later became Wagner's wife. He was always willing to help struggling composers, including Berlioz, Wagner, and Grieg, among others. Liszt helped make Weimar into a highly important art center. In 1865 he took minor orders in the Roman Catholic Church and was referred to as "Abbé Liszt," to the great astonishment of his friends, who remembered his previous escapades. He was a bold innovator, especially in his later years.

Gustav Mahler (1860-1911), *Symphony #1, third movement* (1888)
Mahler was a Jewish, Bohemian-born composer who converted to Roman Catholicism. His music is intensely expressive and highly chromatic. Mahler's work is considered the forerunner of Schoenberg's "Twelve Tone" music. Mahler has a tendency to be long-winded; most of his works have extra-musical links, especially poetry.

This movement of the symphony was inspired by a satirical engraving of *The Hunter's Funeral*, a well-known fairy tale. It is written in three sections (ABA). The A part evokes the funeral-march-beat for the procession; the B part is less serious and uses *Frère Jacques* in a comical and mocking way. He reminds us that the whole affair was nothing but a funeral for a dead hunter by the forest animals.

Fugue

The fugue is a procedure, not a form. It is the systematic exploitation of a theme in strict polyphonic imitation. A fugue can be written for a single instrument (like the organ or harpsichord) or for a group of instruments or voices. It is arguably the most significant legacy of the Baroque Period. Although highly developed in that time, fugal writing never quite disappeared and was used later by Beethoven, Berlioz, Brahms, Stravinsky, Britten, Hindemith, and many other composers. Although every composer has written at least one fugue, it seems very idiomatic of the German composers, for whom music is as much intellect as emotion.

Parts to the fugue are:

1. *Exposition:* subject introduced in all the voices one by one (the only constant feature)

2. *Episode:* modulating passages that separate the various restatements of the theme

Since the fugue is very flexible, no two fugues are the same.

♪ *Featured Music*

J. S. Bach (1685-1750), *Fugue in G minor for Organ (Little Fugue)* **(1709?)**
Bach is unquestionably the grand master of the fugue, although this particular fugue is called "little" by us, not by Bach. The fugue's theme has a distinct singable contour that is skillfully woven through the whole piece. We have hundreds of fugues by Bach, and it is literally impossible to make a choice of which is the fairest.

G. F. Handel (1685-1759), *"For unto Us a Child Is Born"* **from** *The Messiah* **(1741)**
Is it really believable that *The Messiah,* lasting about two and a half hours was written in twenty-four days and that Handel wrote it for those lingering in debtors' prison? Even ignoring all that, Handel's *Messiah* is one of the greatest works in all of music literature.

This piece has basically three themes. The first is the beginning text, *"For unto us a child is born"*; a second theme is edgier and rhythmically more cutting for *"and the government"* and finally, a third, theme, a cry of approval for the *"Wonderful, Counsellor, the Mighty God."* This string of themes is repeated three times with increasing intensity, making it one of the great choral pieces of a most popular oratorio. No wonder that even the King rose to his feet upon hearing the *"Halleluia chorus,"* later in the work.

Although Handel's fugues are not as "strict" and "calculated" as Bach's, his fugal writing is no less effective.

W. A. Mozart (1756-1791), *Symphony #41 (Jupiter)* **(Summer 1788)**
This symphony was the last one Mozart ever wrote. Its title was probably given by an admirer. The last movement, although not a fugue *per se,* reveals an ex-

traordinary ability of fugal writing. It is a superb model of learned contrapuntal writing combined with inspired musicality as only a Mozart could accomplish.

Benjamin Britten (1913-1976), *The Young Person's Guide to the Orchestra, last movement* **(1946)** Britten used a theme of Purcell to make a series of variations demonstrating the different instruments to young people. Just as Bach had done previously in his famous Passacaglia for organ, Britten writes a full-fledged fugue. The theme starts with the piccolo and filters through all voices, one by one. It brings the whole piece to a rousing conclusion.

Britten is an English composer, pianist, and conductor. His stylistic links are Mahler and Stravinsky. He wrote seven operas, lots of chamber music and stacks of choral music. Britten is especially noted for his delightful Christmas music, including *Ceremony of Carols*. He died at sixty-three in London.

Richard Strauss (1864-1949), Also sprach Zarathustra. "Of Science." (1896) Strauss was born in Munich, Germany, but is no relation to the Waltz kings of Vienna (Johann Strauss and his family). He developed the "Symphonic Poem," amongst them, *Don Juan, Till Eulenspiegel*, and others. He wrote at least fifteen operas. Although he lived through the first half of the twentieth century, his music is very much part of the Late-Romantic German School. In *Also Sprach Zarathustra*—"freely after Nietzsche" as the subtitle has it (Nietzsche's book used only the name of the ancient Persian philosopher Zoroaster), Strauss puts the listener into the same frame of mind as someone studying philosophy. The fugue seems to be the right vehicle for this, starting strict at first, then deliberately fragmentary and less focused. Many commentaries have been proposed to this music, but finally it eludes all interpretations since the music is so lucid and attractive that it can be well dispensed of any analysis.

Igor Stravinsky (1882-1971), *Symphony of Psalms, second movement* **(1930)** The ballet *Pulcinella* (Paris 1920) marks the beginning of a new period for Stravinsky: the so-called "neo-classic" style. Stravinsky had been looking at the Baroque Masters for inspiration. Yet it is not an imitation of Bach, but Stravinsky's own linearity of independent voices. This movement has a distinct severe and abstract feel, devoid of all sentimentality and emotion. This work was commissioned for the fiftieth anniversary by the conductor of the Boston Symphony Orchestra. This choral symphony is among Stravinsky's finest compositions, giving the listener an overwhelming impression of religious ecstasy and grandeur.

Expectans expectavi Dominum, et intendi mihi
    I waited patiently for the Lord; and He inclined to me,
Et exaudivit preces meas; et eduxit me de lacu miseriae,
    and heard my cry. He brought me up also out of a
et de luto faecis. Et staquit super petram pedes meos;
    horrible pit, out of the miry clay, and set my feet upon
et direxit gressus meos. Et immisit in os meum canticum
    a rock, and established my goings. And He hath put a
novum, carmen Deo nostro. Videbunt multi et timebunt;
    new song in my mouth, even praise unto our God:
and sperabunt in Domino.
    many shall see it, and hear, and shall trust in the Lord.
                          Psalm XXXIX 1-3 (Vulgate)
                          Psalm XL 1-3 (King James)

Opera

Greek dramas were undoubtedly opera's genesis, although we have no "real" music to prove it. The only evidence are eyewitness accounts. During the Middle Ages, the medieval liturgical Drama, performed in front of the church, was a dramatization of the life of saints, or other religious subjects. Liturgical dance and music were the driving force of the event. Unfortunately, little music is preserved. During the Renaissance, the Florentine Camerata (an intellectual organization which performed theatricals) based their discussions on Girolamo Mei, who concluded that the Greek drama was sung in it entirety. Consequently, they started inserting musical commentaries between the acts of their theater plays.

Claudio Monteverdi, who was acclaimed as a great composer even in his lifetime, composed *Orfeo* in 1607, perhaps the first genuine opera. Although early operas were courtly entertainments, by 1650 they were produced for the general public and became increasingly popular. Even the earliest operas combined all the arts in one single production: painting, sculpture and architecture for the costumes, scenery and background, poetry and drama for the text, and music and ballet to round off the spectacle. Wagner's Gesamtkunst Werk (total art) was there from its inception. Even from day one it proved to be a crowd pleaser, not unlike our own film productions.

♪ *Featured Music*

Claudio Monteverdi (1567-1643), *L'Orfeo, Tu se' morta, mia vita* **(1607)**
Monteverdi, born in Cremona, Italy, was first a choirboy then eventually held several positions in Mantua and finally in Venice, Europe's richest city. He became a priest in 1632, after his wife perished from the bubonic plague. He wrote several operas—his last one when he was seventy-five! He wrote more than 250 madrigals, several masses and two settings of the *Magnificat*. All of his music is vocal, some with instrumental accompaniment, but no purely instrumental pieces were ever found.

This is a highly emotional rendition of Orfeo's lament at the death of his beloved Euridice.

> *You are dead, my life, and I still breathe?*
> *You have left me, never to return, and I remain?*
> *Farewell earth, farewell say and sun, farewell.*

Oratorio

The *Oratorio* is essentially an opera with a biblical text. Acting and/or staging was never involved. The oratorios were especially popular during Lent, when theatrical works and operas were banned. Oratorios had largely the same format as the opera, with recitatives, solo singing and choir intedections. They became most popular in England, especially through the efforts of G. F. Handel. For ordinary Sundays, cantatas were shorter versions of the oratorios, but still built with the same blueprint. Passions, written for Holy Week, were another type of oratorio, based on the Gospel accounts by Matthew, Like, Mark and John of the crucifixion of Jesus Christ. They were written both for Lutheran and Catholic audiences. Next to Handel's *Messiah*, Bach's oratorios and passions are most famous.

♪ *Featured Music*

J. S. Bach (1685-1750), *Cantata #140, Wachet auf, ruft uns die Stimme* **(1731)**
Bach wrote about three hundred cantatas; about 195 are still in existence. He needed one for every feastday and Sunday of the church year. Occasionally, he

reused some works. Most cantatas have several movements; this one has seven. It is based upon the parable of the wise and foolish virgins (Matthew:25).

This widely-known choral tune by Philipp Nicolai provides the basic material for the elaborate opening movement. The slow-moving chorale comes in broken phrases in the soprano, while the rest of the chorus sings quicker notes and the orchestra plays motives from the opening ritornello. After each phrase, the orchestra continues playing interludes based on the initial ritornello. The most exciting moment comes when the whole chorus sings a jubilant *Alleluia*!

G. F. Handel (1685-1759), *Comfort Ye, My People and Every Valley Shall be Exalted (Messiah)* **(1742)** Interestingly, Handel used the tenor only once as soloist in the entire *Messiah*. The first piece is a typical recitativo aria that is less elaborate yet still emphasizes the text; the second piece is more virtuoso and typically bel canto. It opens and closes with a ritornello that permeates the entire movement. There is, as in most arias of that time music tone-painting; for example—the forty-six notes on "exalted," or the rising and falling melody describing the words of every mountain and hill made low. It is sometimes difficult to imagine that Handel performed this work with a small orchestra of strings, harpsichord, two trumpets, and kettledrums accompanied by a men and boys' choir of twenty! Today we perform the same with hundreds of singers and musicians.

Sacred Music

The "Mass" was based on the traditional five sections, i/e the Kyrie, Gloria, Credo, Sancts and Agnus Dei. They are usually massive works written to celebrate special events or holiday services of either Lutheran or Catholic congregations. Requiems have the same format, but usually written for a special person or event. The literature dates to Machaut's *Messe de Notre Dame* in 1364, to Stravinsky's *Mass* in 1948, and Bernstein's *Mass* in 1971. Even several Jazz composers have written masses in their medium. The gamut runs from Palestrina and other Renaissance composers, to Monteverdi, Vivaldi, and Bach in the Baroque Period and Haydn, Mozart and Beethoven in the Classical Period as well as Schubert, Gounod and others in the Romantic Period.

♪ *Featured Music*

Mozart, *Requiem* (1791)

Berlioz, *Requiem* (1837)

Verdi, *Requiem* (1874)

Faure, *Requiem* (1886)

Durufle, *Requiem* (1947)

Andrew Lloyd Webber, *Requiem* (1992)

A most interesting was to study this form is by comparing six Requiems, masses for the dead as practiced in the Roman Catholic church.

Mozart's Requiem began when a mysterious man commissioned a Requiem for his wife, who had died in her early twenties. Mozart had a really tough time working on it, as he had the strange premonition that he was writing his own Requiem. In fact he never did finish the commission, even though he got a handsome down payment for it. This work is serious and quite tragic at times.

Berlioz's Requiem was commissioned by the Secretary of the Interior of France as a Requiem mass for the victims of an assassination attempt upon King Louis-Philippe. Berlioz retained his composure long enough to request five to six hundred musicians, to perform it the way it was in his imagination. At the "Tuba mirum" the effect was so overwhelming that the priest wept openly, women were fainting. The entire work left a highly dramatic impact. Berlioz himself was so pleased that he said, "if ever my entire oeuvre would be burned, I would beg mercy for my Requiem".

Verdi's Requiem: When on May 22, 1873, Alessandro Mazoni died, the greatest poet, novelist, and patriot of that time, Verdi decided to write a fitting tribute for his friend. On the first anniversary of his death it was performed in Manzoni's hometown, Milan. It was Verdi's greatest "opera" as is often referred to. In spite of the chiding tone of some critics it has become one of the great masterpieces of the Romantic era.

Faure's Requiem is, compared to the highly dramatic utterances of Berlioz and Verdi, a most intimate and small-scaled work. Beethoven (who never wrote a Requiem) thought that such a work should be quiet music, without the trump of doom. Faure succeeded in erasing the fear of death with dignity, serenity and brevity. The *In Paradisum* is indeed heavenly music in its simplicity and delicate expression.

Durufle's Requiem is, in the tradition of Faure, serene and transparent. Berlioz apocalyptic vision of the Last Judgment demands multiple brass choruses, a dozen timpani and tam-tams; Durufle omits the Dies frae altogether. The Requiem is essentially based on Gregorian chant, noted for its flexibility in rhythm and simplicity in melody and sincerity of expression.

Andrew Lloyd Webber's Requiem: A Requiem by the composer of *Cats, Evita* and the *Phantom*? Actually Lloyd Webber went to school at Westminster Abbey, so he was familiar with church music, especially since his father had been an organist, not far away at All Saints church. When his father died in 1982 it was natural that Lloyd Webber should write a Requiem in his memory. There is nothing theatrical and he admits that the Requiem is his most austere work to date. The *Pie Jesu* is a heartfelt and very personal expression of acceptance.

Periods of Music

Ancient World to 1000 A.D.

> *Do you want to know if a people have a good life, have*
> *sound morals and good government? Listen to their music.*
> —Confucius (551-479 B.C.)

Music's origins are uncertain as no written accounts are decipherable until about the year 1,000 A. D. While there must have been many attempts in writing down the music, most of the "music" has eluded deciphering even to the most persevering anthropologists and musicologists. Nevertheless, some exciting discoveries of early music instruments and notations have been made.

In 1986-87 New York's American Museum of Natural History displayed a bone carved into a flute by the Cro-Magnons of France, about 30,000 years ago. If correctly dated, this would be the oldest known musical instrument.

Diverse cultures have contributed to music's earlier instruments. In the Ukraine, archaeologists have unearthed what may be early instruments dating from about 20,000 years ago. We have transcriptions of Egyptian music deciphered from hieroglyphic signs from the fourth dynasty (2900-2750 B. C.)—music written with numbers including some "chords" that mark "divine names." Iraq's Sumerians had some rather sophisticated construction of musical instruments, buried with the remains of musicians. They also had richly ornamented lyres and harps used for banquets where diners were entertained with song and dance. Some of their poetry has also been preserved. Even on the Yucatan peninsula, the Mayans developed ocarinas (clay flutes, still available) and drums excavated by a team of National Geographic archaeologists.

Music in Ancient Greece

> *Music is diversion, for educating, for stimulating the spirit*
> *and the soul while liberating the heart of passions.*
> —Aristotle (384-322 B.C.)

In the Greek culture, music has a prominent place within the liberal arts, along with arithmetic, geometry, and astronomy. The Greek philosophers believed that music had magical powers and was capable of influencing people's character and behavior. Greek philosophers wrote extensively about music theory and the place of music in society. During the seventh century B. C. Terpander opened

Greece's first school of music. While the quantity of Greek music must have been enormous, only one brief song and several small fragments have survived.

♪ Featured Music

Seikilos Song, dated anywhere from 200 B. C. to 100 A. D.
"As long as you live, be cheerful; let nothing grieve you, for life is short and time takes its toll." These reflections on the fleeting nature of life were found engraved on the headstone of Seikilos' wife. The music is monophonic, but impressive in its simplicity and purity. Nevertheless the greatness of the ancient Greek civilization is neither in painting nor music, but rather in architecture and sculpture. Only two other pieces, Delphic hymns to Apollo, seem to have survived.

Music in Ancient Rome

The Romans imported both Greek musicians and their music. Brass instruments were adopted from the Etruscans and often used for entertainment and military parades. Musicians were highly regarded and richly rewarded. Cicero (106-43 B. C.) talks about the hydraulic organ making a "delectable sound to the ears." The organ was presumably played at the Coliseum for the gladiators. No trace of either the instrument nor the music remains.

Featured Music

Terence, *Hecyra Verse* 861 (160 B.C.)
Example of Roman music for voice and plucked string instrument. Very similar in style to the Greek music. Little is known about the music of the Roman civilization.

Timeline for The Ancient World

B.C.

30,000	France and Spain, Cro-Magnon had bone flutes
20,000	In Chernigov, Ukraine, drums kettle drums, xylophones
3,800	Egypt; zither, harp, lyre, flute and pan-pipes
2,900	Egypt; music notation dating from fourth dynasty (2,900 - 2,750 B. C.)
2,400	Sumerian poem in praise of music
1,000	Israel: King David's Book of Psalms, believed to be sung
900	Greece: aulos (flute) and Lyra (harp)
675	Greece: Terpander's first School of Music develops; Dorian, Phrygian scales
600	Acropolis built in Athens, Greece
550	Greece: Pythagoras develops a scale built on fifths
350	Socrates fosters the arts, especially poetry and music
350	Aristotle tutors Alexander the Great in philosophy and music
300	Egypt: Hydraulic organ invented by Ktesibios of Alexandria (enjoyed by Cicero)
300	Rome: Hydraulic organ used in the Colosseum
200	Seikilos, musical epitaph for his deceased wife
160	Terence, Hecyra verse
46	Rome: Julius Caesar assassinated on March 15, "the Ides of March"
31	Virgil, Roman poet, wrote twelve books titled "Aeneas" (favorite opera subject)

A.D.

2	World population estimated at 133 million
200	Ambrosian chant used for church (was replaced ca. 600 by Gregorian chant)
313	Constantine allows Christianity in the Empire
330	Roman Empire's capital becomes Constantinople
476	Conquest of Rome by the Goths under Odovacar
600	Reign of Pope Gregory the Great, who codified the chants
711	Moors from Morocco invade Spain; stayed until 1492
800	Charlemagne, first Emperor of the Holy Roman Empire, fosters the Arts
850	Vikings (Norsemen in West; Varangians in East) had a profound influence
900	Alfonso III begins to reconquer Spain from the Moors

Medieval Times (450 to 1450 A.D.)

> *What passion cannot music raise and quell?*
> —John Dryden (1631 -1700)

Early Christian Music

The rise of Christianity created a great need for suitable liturgical music. Until 1300 the Catholic Church organized and developed a vast body of music called Gregorian Chant, eventually codified under the leadership of Pope Gregory the Great (590-604). While many pieces are traced to antiquity, others were added after Gregory I. The nearly three thousand chants in the repertory were used until Vatican II (1963).

♪ Featured Music

Christian Hymn to the Trinity (A. D. 200)
Greek text using the Roman practice of adding instruments.

Gregorian chant: Alleluia, vidimus stellam (Christmas)
"We have seen His star in the East and are coming with gifts to worship the Lord." The full choir sings the Alleluias and the solo choir the verse. It is in the typical ABA form. Melismas are long series of notes on one syllable expressing wordless joy and religious ecstasy, usually reserved for the Alleluias.

First Attempts at Polyphony

By the year 1000 a second part was added to the Gregorian melody. That was called *organum*. At first, the organum moved parallel with the original melody. The originator and place of origin of the organum is unknown, as many countries claim its beginnings. Since writing music was most ambiguous, the answer to the simple proposition, if indeed we know how to perform the chants, is very much open to debate. That is not to diminish the labors of the agonizing musicologists. Nevertheless their speculations never answered this unique phenomenon of the Western hemisphere: the introduction of harmony into the music.

♪ *Featured Music*

Organum: *Sit gloria Domini and Rex coeli* **(ninth century)**
Both pieces are from the Musica Enchiniades, (music handbook) a highly contested medieval treatise of the ninth century. It used Daseian notation derived from ancient Greek poetry. The way this music is presented today, was this really how it was heard during that time? Will we ever know?

Note: Daseian notation, used in 9th and 10th century, was based on ancient Greek poetry.

Hildegard von Bingen (1098-1179), *Plange, Castella misera* **(12th century)**
The visionary Hildegard von Bingen, Benedictine abbess, was a poet and musician having at least 80 vocal works to her name. Recognized by Pope Eugenius as a prophet in 1147, she is one of the most important figures of the Middle Ages. She completed three books of visions, and thirteen works in theology and medicine, as well as over 300 letters to the most powerful leaders throughout Europe. For Hildegard the human soul was a symphony of celestial harmony, produced by human voices and instruments. The visionary Hildegard reveals a mystic universe in which the workings of the cosmic forces take the form of allegoric figures interceding on behalf of the human soul in earthly struggles with the temptations of evil. The music is in the style of the School of Notre Dame. Her music seems to gain in popularity.

Plange, Castella misera,	Lament, O sorrowing Castile;
Plange pro rege Sancio,	lament for Sancho your king
Quem terra, Pontus, ethera	who earth, sea and sky alike
Ploratu plangent anxia.	lament in anxious lament.
Casum tuum considera,	Consider what your state is now,
Patrem plangens in filio,	the father weeps for the son,
Qui, etate tam tenera,	who, at an early age,
Concusso regni solio,	with the throne so shaken,
Cedes sentit st vulnera.	feels a vulnerable wound.

School of Notre Dame

The University of Paris and the Cathedral of Notre Dame, both begun in 1150, attracted many leading scholars and musicians and thus became Europe's intellectual and artistic center. The first notable composers of Paris' Notre Dame School are Leonin and Perotin. Those Notre Dame School composers developed measured rhythms over the free-flowing, unmeasured, elongated Gregorian chant.

♪ Featured Music

Perotin, *Alleluia: Nativitas* (early thirteenth century)
Parisian, composer from the 12th 13ᵗʰ century. He was the successor to Leonin, maître de chapelle of "Notre Dame de Paris" and served in that post from about 1180 to 1230. Leonin's music is exclusively in two-part, whereas Perotin writes frequently in three or even four parts.

The stretched out chant is used as bass, with two quick moving countervoices on top. There may have been some influence of troubadour techniques. Since the music writing is most imprecise, it is difficult to ascertain if indeed that music sounded this way. Perotin's importance can hardly be exaggerated and extends well beyond the beauty and novelty of his compositions.

Secular Music in the Middle Ages

Although Gregorian chant dominated Medieval times, there was also much music outside the church. During this age of chivalry, knights were considered musical poets. Many of their love songs are preserved as they had their clerics write them down. Some 1,650 troubadour and trouvere songs rhythm. In the north of France were the *trouveres*, singing mainly in French (*langue d'ouil*), while in the south of France, the *troubadours* were singing in their mother tongue (*langue d'oc*). At the same time in Germany the Minnesangers took center stage. Those traveling musicians were roaming through Spain, Italy, Austria and Bohemia. Many of the composers are known by name. They usually had harps, fiddles, and lutes for accompaniment. Some names of those wandering knights are: Richard Lionhart, Bernard de Ventadour, Walther von der Vogelweide and Tannhauser. Even St. Francis, who took lady Poverty as his companion, wrote many spiritual songs of praise, poetic pearls in the style of the troubadours.

♪ Featured Music

Walter von der Vogelweide (1170-1230), *Palestine song* (1228)
Born perhaps in Bozen, Tyrol (Austria) and died in Wurzburg, Germany. Of his music little has been preserved, although his contemporaries held him in high

esteem. This song commemorates the Crusade of 1228. *"Only now, since I have come to the place where God walked as man, do I live a true man's life."* The words are embedded in one of the most deeply-felt and refined melodies of that period.

Adam de la Halle (ca. 1240-1286), *The Play of Robin and Marion* **(1284)**
Adam de la Halle was a French trouvere from Arras, northern France, nicknamed *"le bossu,"* the hunchback. The play is known as *Robinhood*. The shepherdess Marion is in love with Robin, but she is courted and abducted by a knight. Robin's rescue fails but in the end Marion persuades the knight to release her. Their reunion is a celebrated in song and dance with their friends.

Numerous attempts have been made to prove that there was a historical Robin Hood, but the ballad is the only evidence of his existence available from the medieval writers. Adam de la Halle was one of the last in a long succession of medieval minstrels. The twelfth song, *Venes après moi (come with me)* closes the popular play. If indeed the tambourine was used is debatable, but it seems appropriate.

Estampie **(thirteenth century dance)**
Only the melody was annotated as was customary. Here it is performed with a rebec, a pear-shaped medieval violin, pipe (flute) and psaltery (harp-like instrument). The accompaniment was probably improvised in those days.

Ars Nova

In the fourteenth century Europe endured the Hundred Years' War (1337-1453) between France and England, then was ravished by the Black Death (about 1350) which claimed at least 60 million lives, perhaps as much as 25% of the population. Meanwhile feudalism and the authority of the church were thus greatly weakened. The Papacy had some serious problems with the First Babylonian Captivity when the Papal See moved from Rome to Avignon, France (1305-1378). The Great Schism (1378-1417), aggravated the situation when rival factions each elected its own Pope.

Literature, including Chauncer's *Canterbury Tales* (1387-1400), stressed realism and sensuality, not virtue and spirituality. Secular music was favored over sacred music. Increasingly composers wrote music which was not based on chant, but on secular poetry. Changes in musical style were so profound that music theorists referred to it as the *Ars Nova*, the "new art."

♪ Featured Music

Guillaume de Machaut (ca.1300-1377), *Messe de Notre Dame* **(1364?)**
The greatest exponent of the *Ars Nova* was Guillaume de Machaut, both a poet and musician. Machaut, born in the diocese of Rheims, France, was a priest who spent most of his life as court official to John, King of Bohemia, accompanying him on European military campaigns. After the king was killed in battle, Machaut became secretary to the royal family of France. Machaut later lived in Rheims as an important churchman. This *Notre Dame Mass* is not only one of the most refined compositions of the Middle Ages, its historical value can hardly be overestimated as it is the first polyphonic treatment for four voices of a complete mass. It may have been composed for the coronation of Charles V at Rheims, but there is no real proof for that.

Guillaume de Machaut (ca. 1300-1377), *Je suis aussi*—**ballad**
At sixty Machaut fell in love with Peronne d'Armentiere, a nineteen-year-old noblewoman. Although priests were allowed to marry at that time, he did not, but still wrote her numerous letters, poems and love songs. Machaut's output is mainly secular songs besides the famous *Notre Dame Mass*. He wrote at least 42 ballads, then a brand new form. He calls them *ballades notees* (ballads with music) as some of his poetry was not intended to be sung. As most music of the troubadours this ballad can be outlined as AAB. It is music from the by-gone world of courtly love.

Je suis aussi com cilz qui est ravis,	I am like one ravished
A	
Qui n 'a vertu, sens ne entendement,	with no strength, sense, or understanding.
Car je suis a nulle riens pensis,	For unceasingly I think of no one else
A	
Jour ne demi, temps, heure ne moment,	every day, all the time, every hour or moment,
Fors seulement a m 'amour	But of my love alone.
B	
Et sans partir en sepenser demour.	I remain in that thought
Soit contre moi, soit pour moy, tout oubli	for or against my will, I forget everything
Fors li qu'aim mieus cent mille fois que mi.	but the one I love a thousand times more than myself

Characteristics of the Medieval Music (Gothic!)

G = Gregorian chant predominates
O = Organuin was the beginning of multi-voiced music
T = Troubadours and trouveres (mostly in France)—secular love-songs
H = Hypothesis as most of the music is unreadable and needs
        scholars to decipher
I = Intellectual and somewhat austere music
C = Clergy are the musicians (the only educated people)

Timeline for the Middle Ages

600-1300	Gregorian chant dominant—named after Pope Gregory 1
604	+ Pope Gregory I (was born in 540)
936-1806	Holy Roman Empire—Romanesque Art at its peak
1000	beginning of the music staff and note singing by Guido of Arezzo
1054	Schism Byzantine<Rome (Orthodox versus Roman Catholicism)
1096	First Crusade (there were 8 until 1270)
1145	Gothic Art at its peak—Chartres and Notre Dame build in Paris
1170	Assassination of Thomas a Becket
1215	Magna Carta, the Great Charter of liberties signed by King John of England.
1226	+ St. Francis
1265	Dante +1321
1266	Giotto, Italian painter +1337
1270	+ St. Louis, King of France died from the plague during the 8th Crusade
1274	+ St. Thomas Aquinas, great theologian
1280	*Sumer is icumen*, the oldest known canon for four voices and two bass voices
1291	Muslims retake Palestine
1300	Guillame de Machaut +1377, composer of the famous Notre Dame mass
1304	Petrarca + 13 74 1305 Popes reside in Avignon, France, until 1377
1340	Chaucer + 1400
1337	Beginning of the "Hundred Years War" between France and England
1347	Black Death claims 60 million (25% of the population)
1354	Turks begin their European invasion

1364	Machaut's *Mass of Notre Dame* (first polyphonic mass)
1368	Clavichord, first keyboard popular in Germany
1386	*Canterbury Tales* written by Chaucer
1400	Dufay, Flemish composer in service of Burgundy + 1474
1401	Famous Baptistry doors sculpted in Florence by Ghiberti
1415	French defeated by Henry V at Agincourt
1427	Thomas a Kempis, influential spiritual writer.
1431	Joan of Arc burned as a witch, at the stake in Rheims
1438	Gutenberg invents moveable type printing
1442	Donatello sculpts his famous "David"
1450	Gunpowder invented; this meant the end of armor and spears.

The Renaissance (1450-1600)

*I am strongly persuaded that after theology there is no art that
can be placed on a level with music; for besides theology, music
is the only, art capable of affording peace and joy of the heart...
the devil flees before the sound of music almost as much
as before the Word of God.*

—Martin Luther

Flourishing between 1450 and 1600, the Renaissance is considered Europe's apex of civilization. Novelist Marsilio Ficino in 1492 characterized the Renaissance as "a golden age" restoring "to light the liberal arts which were almost extinct: grammar, poetry, painting, sculpture, architecture, music." It was a triumphal time for the arts.

During the Renaissance the very idea of "Europe" acquired a widely understood significance, appreciated as the singular culture that had a unique understanding of the valued aspects of civilized life. In the 20th century, the Renaissance historian John Hale has written that the age "witnessed the most concentrated wave of intellectual and cultural energy that had yet passed over the continent" and that it "was a period in which there were such dramatic changes of fortune for better or worse—religious, political, economic and, through overseas discoveries, global—that more people than ever before saw their time as unique, referring to it as 'this new age.'"

At the very center of this new age was the Catholic Church, although weakened through internal strife, nevertheless empowered and supported this new melding of Christianity and classicism in the arts. The church helped marry the best that had been thought and said in antiquity with the passion of Catholic belief The result was an age that did not forfeit its faith, but rather found a new way to incorporate the rebirth and rediscovery of the genius of antiquity.

While air has taken its toll on the ceilings of the Sistine Chapel and the remarkable frescoes of the great cathedrals of Europe, high-minded librarians through the ages have kept the beautiful hand-painted illuminated books out of the sunlight and out of the public's reach. There, between the pages of thousands of manuscripts, resides the glory and beauty that was once the Italian Renaissance.

With Johann Gutenberg's invention of printing 1438, and the subsequent emerging printing industry, books (many with music) were more widely available and affordable to the rising monies merchant class. Printed music greatly improved the notation of music, as printing demanded greater uniformity and precision. While Leonardo Da Vinci and Michelangelo were both known principally as painters, sculptors, and architects - they were also recognized as musicians. This ideal extended to women as well, who, while not permitted to sing in church choirs, were virtuoso singers at several Italian courts and public operas during the late Renaissance. Indeed the Renaissance ideal noted that the "universal man" was to be musically trained. "I am not pleased with the courtier if he not be also a musician," wrote Castiglione in *The Book of the Courtier* (1528). Shakespeare calls for music in his stage plays over 300 times, and his dramas are full of musical references.

> *The man that hath no music in himself,*
> *Nor is not moved with concord of sweet sounds,*
> *Is fit for treasons, stratagems and spoils.*
> —(The Merchant of Venice—Shakespeare)

In music, the term 'Renaissance' is difficult to apply since the rediscovery of Greek music was not possible, as there was a lack of credible models. The revival in the visual arts and literature was more obvious. Thus the most satisfactory definition for the music in the Renaissance should be pursuit in the stylistic qualities of clarity, balance, well-established rules and codes that resulted in a product worthy of the high standards of the humanists. The eminent French Palestrina scholar J. Samson said it best as he states "Palestrina ou la poèsie de l'exactitude," Palestrina is the poet of precision.

The leading school of the Renaissance was called the Flemish School, as most of the leading members were born in Flanders (Brussels, Antwerp, etc.) and the northern France (Arras, Cambrai, Lille). These composers seldom stayed in their home-country and most held prominent positions with church choirs and in the chapels of kings princes. Because of this, the Flemish School had an international dimension of great influence. In the second half of the 16th century we have unique interaction of the Flemish teachers with their foreign pupils.

The great innovation of the Flemish School was the consistent use of four part writing, resulting in a truly polyphonic style enhanced by imitation, the dominant factor in voice equivalence. It became the ideal music for the church with its free-flowing prose rhythm, serene quality and beauty of the inner voices. Although the Church always was apprehensive of music other than Gregorian Chant, the Flemish polyphonic School was proclaimed as a worthy alternative.

♪ *Featured Music*

Josquin des Pres (1450-1521), *Ave Maria* **(1497)**
It is difficult to retrace the checkered career of Josquin. But one thing is clear—that Josquin, even in his lifetime, was considered a musical genius. He worked in many places and even his severest Italian critics declaimed "ho dovuto esclamare bello," "we had to cry out how beautiful." His music has the unique quality of combining the learned contrapuntal ingenuity as means to a higher end—the musical expression of feeling.

Palestrina (1525-1594), *Missa Papae Marcelli,* **Kyrie (1590)**
Giovanni Pierluigi da Palestrina took his name from the hill town known in Roman time as Preneste. He seldom used his family name, Pierluigi. In 1551 he was appointed *organista e maestro di canto* at St. Peter's Basilica in Rome, where he stayed until his death. His burial at St. Peter's gives proof of the high esteem bestowed the "Princeps Musicae," the Prince of Music. The list of compositions attributed to Palestrina is staggering—some 93 masses and 600 motets, as well as a vast number of secular works. According to his own words he worked slowly and the "polished" (his own words) perfection of these masterpieces were not the result of haste and speed but rather of careful study and revision. Palestrina is the logical successor to, and culmination of, the Flemish School. Palestnina's Pope Marcellus Mass was always believed to be the standard for polyphonic masses at the Council of Trent, although not it is no longer accepted to have been such a model.

Roland de Lassus (1532-1594*), Matona, mia cara* **Madrigal (undated)**
Lassus was born in Flanders and died in Munich, Germany, in the same year as
Palestrina. After traveling through Italy he settled permanently in Munich. With
his over 2000 works, he can be called the most prolific composer of all time: he
was even more productive than Bach! He is not an innovator (neither was Bach)
but a genial resume of what the Renaissance had offered so far in music. Besides
an enormous amount of church music his output in the madrigal genre is impressive. The secular pieces give Lassus the opportunity to express *joie de vivre*
and vivid picturesque scenes, that still give many madrigal choir a great deal of
pleasure. The recurring "don, don, don, dire don, don, don" is not only an essential element of the rondo form, but also a subtle imitation of a drum. Matona
is unquestionably a misspelling of Madonna, mia cara—My dear girl. The text is
a curious mixture of broken Italian and Bavarian German.

Thomas Weelkes (1575-1623), *As Vesta Was Descending* **(1601)**
Weelkes was born and died in London, England and became organist of the
famous Chichester Cathedral, a post he held until his untimely death. The madrigals were not practiced in Italy alone, but were prolific in Elizabethan England
as well. We have dozens of names, although Weelkes holds very high rank; some
even proclaiming him the greatest of them all.

This madrigal is typical of the light mood of the English madrigals. Most remarkable is the clever word painting. There are plenty of examples: the word
descending is sung to downward scales, the word *ascending* to upward scales.
At the words *"two by two"* then *"three by three together"* and later their goddess all
"alone" the music replies in turn. At the words *"Long live Oriana"* the bass sings
with "long" notes, while the other voices imitate in joyful affirmation. This madrigal was written to honor Queen Elizabeth, who was often called Oriana.

As Vesta was from Latmos hill descending,	descending scales
she spied a maiden queen the same ascending,	ascending scales
attended on by all the shepherds swain,	
to whom Diana's darlings	
came running down amain.	rapid descending scales
First two by two,	two voices
then three by three together,	three voices, then all together

leaving their goddess all alone, hasted thither,   solo voice
and mingling with the shepherds of her train
with mirthful tunes her presence entertain.
Then sang the shepherds and nymphs of Diana,
Long live fair Oriana!   long bass notes—generally
     joyful

Instrumental Music During the Renaissance

The music of the Renaissance, although for a great percentage vocal, has never-theless a great amount of instrumental music. A favorite was the lute, a guitar-like instrument shaped like a half pear, useful for accompaniments. In addition we have a whole family of viols, gambas and the beginnings of the clavier, in the form of the clavichord and eventually the harpsichord, especially after 1500. The organ also became a prominent instrument, as were diverse brass instru-ments used for playing hymns from the church tower.

Most of the instrumental music was intended for dancing. Most dances come in pairs, a step dance and a jumping dance. In France the *Basse-dance* was paired with a *Tourdion,* or a *Pavane* with a *Gaillarde*; in Italy a *Padovana* was paired with a *Saltarello*: and in Germany an *Allemande* was coupled to a *Hupfauf*.

If initially instruments played similar music as the vocal counterpart—canzona became a ricercar—the first one for voices and the second for instruments, the instrumental music became more and more independent and no longer relied on vocal models. Especially on the keyboards, composers developed purely in-strumental forms, such as theme and variations, preludes and toccatas. Since every cultivated person was expected to be an accomplished dancer, much dance music was published during the sixteenth century, most of it with only the melody line as the accompaniments and drum parts were improvised. Today's rendi-tions may only be at best conjecture; nevertheless we have some believable re-cordings. Most indoor instruments had a much softer sound, and most instruments, including the viols and recorder flutes, came in families ranging from soprano to bass. The nasal krummhorns—precursor to the bassoon—held the bass part. The outdoor instruments, the trumpets, trombones, and shawms (ancestor to the oboe) were rather loud and shrill.

The Renaissance composers left the choice of instruments to the performers. The average consort, or small band of musicians, at the courts was about ten, playing diverse instruments. Only for state occasions such as royal weddings or state funerals was a greater group assembled, playing bowed instruments, with keyboard and perhaps some brass chorus.

Besides the abundance of dance music we cannot overlook the growing English Virginal School. The virginal was a type of harpsichord, perhaps named after the virga (wooden jacks) not because virgins play on them." Most of their music came down to us through the so-called *My Ladye Nevells Booke* (1591), containing 42 compositions by William Byrd, and the Fitzwilliam Virginal Booke, containing 297 compositions from practically every composer of that time—a treasure of music that without it would have never reached us. The most important names are John Bull, Orlando Gibbons, and the aforementioned William Byrd.

The greatest surprise of the English Virginal School is in their originality: the strict voice leading style is washed out; nothing reminds us of a vocal blueprint. The style is purely based on a finger technique, endemic to the instrument: rapidly repeated notes, fast moving figures, crossovers for the hand all lead to a rich future. That future, by way of the early Baroque masters like Sweelinck and Buxtehude, will lead to Bach and Handel. There is a vast amount of recordings available (see the extensive list of suggested recordings especially under "the Renaissance").

Speaking of books, an unexpected source of Renaissance music is no less than the son of Christopher Columbus. Ferdinand was the son of Columbus' mistress, whom he never married, perhaps since she was a peasant girl. In 1502 Ferdinand accompanied his father on his fourth voyage to the New World. On his return Ferdinand developed a taste for good books and music. He became wealthy, through especially the revenue from 400 slaves in the New World. He used his wealth to purchase books and manuscripts and his library included more than 15,000 books, many exclusively music. About 2,000 volumes have survived and are today located at the Seville Cathedral. The *Biblioteca Columbina* still preserves the *Cancionero* musical, an invaluable source of Renaissance music, that had been among Ferdinand's possessions.

Characteristics of the Renaissance Art and Music

<u>H</u> = Humane and gentle, in contrast to the austere character of Medieval Music

<u>U</u> = Universities replaced monasteries as a course of learning

<u>M</u> = Madrigals in mother tongue, rather than Latin

<u>A</u> = A capella; most church music restricted to voices only.

<u>N</u> = Names used (mostly first name and city origin, for example Giovanni da Palestrina)

<u>I</u> = International flavor: music and all other arts have a universal character

<u>S</u> = Sacred and secular art and music, while still linked, are increasingly separated.

<u>M</u> = Masculine world. Although women could be performing artists.

Renaissance Timeline

1450-1600	Flemish School, had international ramifications
1452	Leonardo da Vinci + 1519
1453	Fall of Constantinople to the Turks
1456	Bible printed by Gutenberg
1469	Lorenzo Medici elected Duke of Florence—the Renaissance is at its peak
1473	Copernicus + 1543
1475	Michelangelo +1564
1477	Spanish Inquisition ordered by King Ferdinand and Queen Isabella
1477	Botticelli paints the *Primavera*
1483	Raphael + 1520 Rome, Painter of Vatican
1485	Bosch paints his *Garden of Earthly Delights*
1485	Titian + 1576 most prominent painter of his day
1492	Columbus discovers the New World
1495	Da Vinci paints the *Mona Lisa* and *The Last Supper*
1500	Charles V in Ghent, Belgium. Emperor of the Holy Roman Empire
1501	First book of printed music in Florence, Italy
1506	Michelangelo starts St. Peters Basilica in Rome, under Pope Julius
1512	Michelangelo paints the Sistine Chapel
1513	Ponce de Leon discovers Florida
1511	Erasmus writes his *Praise of Folly*
1515	Machiavelli writes *The Prince*
1517	Luther starts the Reformation

1519	da Vinci dies 2 May 1519—Cortez begins conquest of Mexico
1534	The Jesuit order begins the Counter-Reformation
1534	Henry VIII declares himself head of the Church of England
1541	De Soto discovers the Mississippi River
1563	Council of Trent (Church music laws enacted)
1558	Elizabeth I becomes Queen of England, great patron of the arts and music
1560-1620	English Virginal School
1572	St. Bartholomew's Eve Massacre in France against the Protestants
1587	Mary Queen of Scots executed
1588	Drake defeats the Spanish Armada (Spain never regained its former power)
1590	St. Peter's Basilica finished by Michelangelo
1592	Columbus in the Bahamas
1601	Shakespeare's *Hamlet*

The Baroque Period (1600-1750)

Music is the answer to the mystery of life. It is the most profound of all the arts: it expresses the deepest thoughts of life and being in simple language which nonetheless cannot be translated.
—Arthur Schopenhauer

Keywords to describe the Baroque are magnificence, opulence and grandeur. It was a great time to be alive. Opportunities for artists increased in music as well as in the other arts and sciences. Painting reached new heights of perfection and imagination. Sculpture became more expressive than ever. The emphasis shifted from craftsmanship to expression. Architecture stressed luxuriant splendor, grandiose concepts, and majestic design. The arts were collectively brilliant and luxurious, reflecting a spectacular time of optimism and bustling, even volcanic action. Artists such as Bernini, Rubens, and Rembrandt exploited their materials to expand the potentials of details, colors, ornaments, and depth; totally structured worlds of illusion. Such a style was perfect for the wishes of the aristocracy. In France, Louis XIV held court in the Palace of Versailles, a magnificent structure that married painting, sculpture, and architecture into a symphony of royal wealth and power.

The Baroque style with its theatrical qualities also enters the church, making the houses of worship more attractive and appealing. The churches' interiors became more dramatic, with baldacchinos over the altars, ornate pulpits, with a parade of sculptures and a richly displayed organcase in the choirloft. Stone was sculpted into soft forms to look like plaster; plaster was made to resemble wood; wood was polychromed to look like bronze; bronze was glided to look like gold; gold was encrusted with precious stones; and walls were painted to look like marble. All of this ostentatiousness reflected magnificent pomp and daring virtuosity in their artistry. As Louis IV wrote "My dominant passion is certainly love of glory" could easily be applied to the opulence and triumphalism of the churches.

Yet, in many ways it was a period of great sanctity in the Roman Catholic Church almost equal to the twelfth century. Ignatius Loyola, Theresa of Avila, Filipo Neri and Francis Xavier were all canonized on the same day, 22 May 1622. Rome felt regenerated after the disastrous Reformation of Luther.

The middle class, mostly prosperous merchants, commissioned portraits and landscapes to adorn their interiors and display their wealth, especially in Holland. Amsterdam was the first center of bourgeois capitalism. It had become, since the decline of Antwerp and the Hanseatic League, the great port and banking center of the North. Holland can boast more than a handful of painters, but indisputably the greatest of them is Rembrandt van Rijn (1609-1669). For twenty years just about every Dutch painter was his pupil. Rembrandt was the great poet painter, who produced the first visual and expressive translation of the Bible. Just as much as Dante, Michelangelo, Shakespeare, Newton and Goethe, Rembrandt and Rubens are to some extent a kind of summation of their time.

Science too made some great discoveries during the seventeenth century. The new approach of mathematics and experiment, as exemplified by Galileo (1564-1642) and Newton (1642-1727) led to improvements and new inventions in medicine, mining, navigation, and industry that made many cities and merchants prosper. The Baroque period is a complex mixture of rationalism, sensuality, materialism, and spirituality. This created a duality of extravagance held in check by a systematic intellectual control. A boisterous Toccata followed by a learned Fugue is the perfect analogy.

During the Baroque period life became more and more secularized. The production of secular music easily surpassed sacred music's output. Even sacred music developed a secular slant minimizing the difference between the two. People's greater interest in human rather than religious expression created a fascination with theater and opera. Hearing an opera and hearing an oratorio differed only in the texts used. While the Renaissance maintained the spirit of restraint, the Baroque extravagance permeated everywhere.

Playing a polyphonic mass by Palestrina next to the Gloria by Monteverdi, (written as part of a special Mass at St. Mark's on November 28, 1631) is like night and day. Palestrina's music was written with great control, and essentially for a cappella choir, whereas Monteverdi's Gloria was written for a seven-part choir, organ, trombones, trumpets and strings. Every time the work "Gloria" sounds, trailing clouds of melodic exultation appear with immeasurable jubilation. Palestrina's music is mystical and serene, while Monteverdi rather gives an eloquent oration for the same event. And yet the two works are chronologically separated by a mere forty years (1590 versus 1631).

The output of Baroque music was enormous. Writing music was no longer-problematic, thanks to the demands of the printers. Even the handwritten manuscripts can be read by a 20th century performer. The composers invented a shorthand for the harmony, called figured bass, which increased the speed of their dexterous writing. The Baroque, originally started in Venice, spread rapidly into Germany, especially as of 1640. Germany would eventually produce two of the period's musical giants, Bach and Handel. Bach became the apex of the Baroque in Germany itself, while Handel carried the torch into England. The splendors of the Baroque permeated the music of France as well, especially through Couperin, Lully and Rameau. Although the French never practiced the erudite intricacies of the fugue, canon and other cerebral utterances of the Germanic composers, their music in no less dazzling, well-liked and versatile. The Baroque was also evident in Italy; Vivaldi, Scarlatti and Corelli make a unique trio—ready to export their wares to an eager England.

Italy's greatest contribution to the Baroque was the opera. What began around 1600 as a serious attempt to recapture the spirit of the classic Greek drama evolved, by mid-century, into a spectacle of bel-canto built around heroes and heroines of Roman and Greek legends—Orpheus, Poppea, Daphne, Andromeda. Soon the Italian opera was soon marketed in France, Austria, Germany and England and made it all the way to St. Petersburg, a long way from home.

If Da Vinci is said to be the consummate Renaissance man, it would be difficult to squeeze the whole Baroque into one single human being. For one thing, the Baroque was cultivated for such a long period and many artists put their own indelible stamp on its style. Any single person that is meant to sum up the aesthetic tendencies of 150 or so years is bound to be inadequate. Who is going to select the greatest among Bach, Handel, Telemann, Couperin, Lully, Rameau, Vivaldi, Scarlatti, Rembrandt, Velazquez, Jordaens, Van Dyck, Rubens, Milton, Dryden, Shakespeare, Bernini or Sir Christopher Wren? There is no doubt that in that glorious century the appeal to reason and expression was a triumph for the human intelligence.

♪ *Featured Music*

Claudio Monteverdi (1567-1643), *Gloria* (1631)
Originally written for a thanksgiving mass for the cessation of the plague which raged for over a year, killing tens of thousands. Monteverdi and his son Francesco were spared, although St. Mark's lost several of her musicians. It was written for a service as part of a special mass at St. Mark's on November 28, 163 1. He uses a seven-part choir, organ, trombones and strings. It is no longer Renaissance polyphony, but the birth of Baroque glory.

After the initial exuberant *"Gloria"* there is a sudden contrast at the words *"Et in terra pax hominibus"* (and peace to his people on earth) shifting form the exultant to the prayerful and introspective. At *"Qui tollis peccata mundi"* two sopranos together with a solo bass (you take away the sin of the world) sing one of the most moving passages of the work. *"Tu solus Altissimus"* (you alone are the most high) gives the incentive for the high notes in all voices.

The final section *"In Gloria Dei Patris. Amen"* reiterates the initial joyfulness and exuberant feeling. It is a magnificent expression of hope and optimism.

Claudio Monteverdi, *L'Incoronazione di Poppea* (1642)
All essential ingredients for an opera are already in place: the overture, the recitative (the actual story telling), the aria (the emotional reflection to the story), the chorus (often representing the crowds) and Ballet (a diversion to the drama at hand). Monteverdi assigns the role of a hero to the tenor and heroines usually are taken by the soprano. Through the ages that format will change only little. Although still in infancy the operas by Monteverdi were conceived with a full deck.

The opera *L'Incoronazione di Poppea* was first performed at the Theatro di Santi Giovanni e Paolo in Venice, in the autumn of 1642, when the composer was 75! The opera is based on events that may have taken place when Nero was Emperor. The libretto by Busenello is based on historical fact, but elaborates with generous poetic license to make the story more palatable to the public. In this opera, the crown jewel of a long career, Monteverdi poured some of his most inspired music, making it one of the masterpieces of the Italian Baroque. It was his swansong.

The overture is rather short, but very dignified, with the air of royalty. In the first scene, we find Nero with Poppea in the bedroom. The music takes a very drastic turn. From a rather exalted prelude, the music suddenly deteriorates to a flimsy and frivolous accompaniment for Poppea's storyline. When Nero replies, the music regains some composure and mills and frills are momentarily omitted. But when Poppea continues her demands the music underlines her stern and irrevocable demand to kill Nero's counselor, the philosopher Seneca, who was against this illicit proposition. The music follows closely the different emotions within the scene. The opera has some deeply moving passages, not the least when Seneca's pupils are begging him not take his own life. At the end trumpets join in celebrating the Coronation. A grandiose hymn of praise by the chorus of consuls and tribunes leads to the climax of the opera. The final love duet is one of the most beautiful ever composed. Monteverdi sustains the latter melody with a typical "passacaglia" bass.

Henry Purcell (1659-1695), *Dido's Lament* Recitativo and Aria (1689)
Purcell lived all his life in London. Rather young he became the organist for Westminster Abbey. It is said that he died through a cold caused by being locked out of his house at night. Who was responsible?

Purcell's reputation always was high and even today has influenced several English composers. Only Handel was able to take over from England's Glory.

In 1689 Purcell wrote this opera for a Chelsea girl's school. Most of us today would consider this perhaps a bit heavy duty for High School girls. The story is well known and from Virgil's hand (Roman poet 70-19 B. C.). Aeneas, the defeated king of the Trojans, was ordered by the gods to look for a new country. He sets out with twenty-one ships and lands at Carthage, a North African port city. Dido, the queen of that city, falls in love with Aeneas and a sorceress and her accomplices see this as an opportunity to plot Dido's downfall. Some false gods command Aeneas to leave Carthage and go on with the search for a new country.

Dido feels betrayed and refuses Aeneas' offer to stay. After he sails, Dido calls her companion Belinda and confides to her of her intent to kill herself.

The recitativo, with its low melodic profile, sets a sorrowful tone. In the aria Purcell put great emotional emphasis in the melody as Dido pours out her soul's reflection. The aria is built upon a "passacaglia" of eight descending chromatic tones. Did Purcell ever hear Monteverdi's melodies built on a similar passacaglia bass as he did in Orfeo?

Recitative:
Thy hand, Belinda; darkness shades me,
On thy bosom let me rest;
More I would, but Death invades me;
Death is now a welcome guest.

Aria:
When I am laid in earth, may my wrongs
create no trouble, no trouble in thy breast,
Remember me! Remember me!
But ah! forget my fate.

Archangelo Corelli (1653-1713), *Concerto fatto per la notte di natale* **(1712)**
Corelli was born near Bologna and died in Rome (was buried in the Pantheon next to Raphael, the famous painter). It is not too strong to call him the father of the violin literature, as no one before him knew how to put as much pathos in his violin sonatas. The year before his death he published 12 concerti grossi, one of which is this exquisite Christmas concerto. Especially the second movement is of exceptional quality.

Antonio Vivaldi (1678-1741), *La Primavera* **from** *The Four Seasons* **(1725)**
Vivaldi, the "prete rosso" "red Priest," is from Venice. His father, Giovanni Baptista, was a prominent violinist, and his son, even though a priest, would write hundreds of concertos for violin, flute, oboe, bassoon, mandolin and at least 39 operas. Although some works seem repeats of previous composition, nevertheless Bach had the highest esteem for Vivaldi's craft and copied and arranged several concertos for organ and some for harpsichord. Most of the concertos were written for his Ospedali della Pieta, a school for orphaned and illegitimate girls, who otherwise may have ended up drowning in the canals. At least 40 girls were involved in the orchestra.

As are most of the concertos, the *Four Seasons* are built on the Rondo principle. The ritornello (refrain) is a short happy tune that is interrupted by first "the song of birds," later the "murmuring streams," then by "thunder and lightening" and lastly by the return of the "bird songs." Especially the scenes of the birds and the storms are most realistic and full of tone paintings, albeit a bit naive for our ears. All the "seasons" have three movements—fast, slow, fast.

The *Spring* Concerto was as popular in his day as it is today. It was a special favorite of Louis XV, king of France, who asked for it as an encore again and again.

Since Vivaldi was so popular and well liked, why then did he suddenly leave Venice for the greener pastures of Vienna, only to die there in poverty shortly after his arrival? This will remain a mystery.

Antonio Vivaldi: *La Primavera* (Spring) from his *Four Seasons* OP. 8, NO. 1 composed in 1725.

First Movement: Allegro

Baroque Ritornello form (Rondo). Scored for solo violin, string orchestra, harpsichord

0.00	A. Tutti, ritornello consisting of two phrases, both repeated p
0.30	B. Solo violin, imitating song of the birds
1.03	A. Tutti, ritornello closing phrase only.
1.10	C. violins p, running notes in cellos suggesting sailing on the Adriatic
1.33	A. Tutti, ritornello closing phrase only.
1.40	D. string tremolos, with sudden upwards running scales, answered by cellos tremolos suggesting Thunder and Lightning.
2.06	A. Tutti, ritornello closing phrase in minor key.
2.13	E. Return to "Song of Birds" in minor key this time.
2.30	A. Tutti, ritornello opening phrase ending in major key.
2.40	F. Continuation of "Song of Birds"
2.54	A. Tutti, ritornello closing phrase, with repeat p.

J. S. Bach (1685-1750), *Toccata and Fugue in D minor* **(dated perhaps 1720)**
Blessed year of 1685—three of the greatest composers of the Baroque (of all time?) were born: Bach, Handel and Scarlatti, and that two years after Rameau! Orphaned early, Bach studied with his older brother and soon was organist in Lüneburg, later in Arnstadt, Mulhausen and finally in Weimar. At least in the latter city he stayed 19 years. He was put under house arrest for 40 days for wanting to leave for Cöthen, which he ultimately did. There he stayed 6 years to eventually leave for Leipzig, where he died after 27 years of service as Director of Music for four churches. Bach himself had at least twenty children by two wives, taught numerous students who provided music for the churches, while he composed all the music for the Sunday services. A busy man! This gigantic undertaking only brought the best out of him, and his music was always hum-

bly signed "J. J." Jesu juva—Jesus help and prefaced with AMDG: *Ad majorem Deum gloriani*—for the fostering of God's glory.

When Bach wrote this Toccata and Fugue is not clear, but most likely when he was in Weimar.

The Toccata expresses youthful exuberance, strength and vitality—the fugue is relatively free of cerebral counterpoint and has some playful passages that exploit the echoes produced by the different stops and manuals. This virtuosity, diversity, mingled with a healthy amount of pathos. Although Bach wrote dozens of fugues, this piece remains a favorite for many listeners.

Johann Sebastian Bach: Toccata *in d minor*

Its original date is uncertain, although we can readily assume that at least the toccata was written by a younger Bach. The more mature fugue may have been added at a later date.

The piece has all the characteristics of the capricious Baroque. It is dazzling and with more than a handful of virtuoso display. Thundering chords over a profound pedal crash creates a study in contrasts and creative imagination. No wonder it remains one of Bach's most beloved compositions.

J. S. Bach, *Brandenburg Concerto #5 in D Major, first movement*
With this set of six concertos Bach brought immortality to an ungrateful German aristocrat, the Margrave of Brandenburg, who never acknowledged its arrival let alone its dedication to him. The concertos are written in the prevailing Concerto Grosso style and the first movement uses the customary Rondo form. The ritornellos (refrains) are constantly interrupted by virtuoso passages of soloing flute or violin, sometimes in competition, sometimes by themselves, but always brilliant and imaginative. Towards the end the harpsichord is assigned a lengthy solo section. The solo part is most demanding and requires a very skillful player of the highest order. Audiences are still in adoring wonder at the challenges of the piece. Why did Bach write those concertos? Was he submitting a resume for a vacant job offered by Christian-Ludwig of Brandenburg? Why then did the latter not even open the package?

Georg Friedrich Handel (1685-1759), *Ev'ry valley shall by exalted,* **aria (1742)**
Just as Bach cannot be captured with only a couple of examples, Handel also will be shortchanged by a couple of pieces. Although Bach and Handel were born in the same year and nearly in the same neck of the woods, their lives were vastly different. For one thing, Handel was better schooled and attended the University with the intent to become a lawyer. Soon the opera was to be his ticket to wealth and fame. He studied in Italy and soon, in 1710 he was in London hawking his *Rinaldo,* an Italian opera that he had ready in fourteen days! The ambitious Handel was ready for the world and even though he had left Hanover under a cloud of difficulties with the local Duke, he soon found himself subject to George 1, his former boss! But the diplomatic Handel soon reconciled (allegedly by wooing the King with his *Water Music Suite*).

Around 1740 Handel grew more interested in the oratorio. He leaves the ungrateful Londoners, who were no longer interested in his operas. Handel went to Ireland where he was hailed as a king with his *Messiah*. He did return to London and lived there venerated as a national glory. His fortune he distributed to the less fortunate. Handel died on Easter Saturday 1759 and was buried in Westminster Abbey. Strangely enough Bach and Handel never met, and yet they are usually mentioned in the same breath.

"and ev'ry, mountain and hill made low, the crooked straight and the rough places plain." (Isaiah 40:4). This passage contains vivid tone painting. For instance the words "low," and "straight," both get special treatment, and the word "exalted" boast forty-six rapidly ascending notes, expressing extreme joy and excitement. Interestingly this is the only aria for tenor!

The Messiah is and will be a perennial favorite, not only because the King at the time stood up for that rousing, enthusiastic Halleluia chorus but for the many familiar melodies connected with the sacred story.

G. F. Handel (1685-1759), *Royal Fireworks* **(1749)**
Besides the famous *Watermusic* from the early 1730's, Handel's most popular orchestral music is the music for the Royal Fireworks. In the spring of 1749 Handel was commissioned to supply suitable music for the signing of the Treaty of Aachen, which ended the War of the Austrian Succession. For the fireworks an enormous platform was erected according to the plans of the stage designer Servandoni.

The performance was not an unqualified success; an uninvited steady drizzle set in and the pavilion caught fire. This was too much for Signot Servandoni, who drew his sword on the hapless Mr. Charles Frederick "Comptroller of His Majesty's Fireworks as well for War and Triumph." He was promptly jailed!

The music itself, written in the French manner, was performed by a band of 100 musicians." The five movements must have been a great asset to the festivities, even though spoiled by rain and strife!

> **G.F. Handel:** *Hornpipe* **from the** *"Water music"* **Third Suite (early 1730s)**
>
> A B A form
>
> 0:00   A section is mainly brass, in ensemble and duet.
> 0:58   B section is devoted to the strings, giving the brass a rest.
> 1:55   return of A section again given to the brass ensemble.

Characteristics of Baroque Art and Music

B = Bach, Handel, Vivaldi, Purcell; painters like: Rembrandt, Rubens, Velasquez
A = Action filled; aristocratic feel in music and all the other arts
R = Rhythm steady, with continuous perpetual motion
O = Optimistic, upbeat and exuberant
Q = Quantity output but with quality input in all the arts.
U = Unity of mood within one single piece. (what is happy stays happy, etc.)
E = Expressive, emotional especially in the opera and all the other arts

Timeline 1600-1750

1593	Thermometer invented
1599	Velasquez, + 1660 Spanish painter
1600	British in Virginia, Dutch in Manhatten
1607	First Opera: Monteverdi's "Orfeo"
1608	Milton, + 1676, author of Paradise Lost (written 1663)
1609	Telescope invented
1609	Henry Hudson navigates the Hudson river

1611	King James Bible
1613	Romanov, Czars in Russia (until 1917)
1614	+ El Greco at 73
1616	+ Shakespeare at 52
1620	Mayflower in Plymouth, Mass.
1622	Moliere, + 1673 at 51
1623	Pascal, + 1662 at 39
1632	Vermeer, + 1675, Dutch painter dies at 43
1640	+ Peter Paul Rubens at 63, Flemish painter
1643	Newton, + 1727 at 84
1643	Louis XIV King of France for 72 years (encouraged the arts greatly)
1644	Antonion Stradivarious + 1737, Italian violin-maker, produced 1,116 violins
1649	Guarneri, rival to Stradivarius in violin-making
1660	Electric generator
1664	Bubonic plague kills 75,000 in London
1666	Great fire in London destroys 13,000 houses, 84 churches, St.
1666	Calculus developed
1666	+ Frans Hals, Dutch painter, at 86
1669	French Academy of Music founded
1672	Peter the Great, Czar to 1725 (53 years) (fosters greatly the arts)
1684	+ Arnati, Italian violinmaker, at 86
1692	Salem Witch trials in New England
1701	Queen Anne in England (elegant furniture style named after her)
1705	Steam pump invented by Newcomen, will lead to Watt's steam engine (1769)
1710	Christofori invents the piano, which Bach appraised
1714	Handel's Water Music played in London for King George I, his patron
1714	"Four Seasons" composed by Vivaldi
1718	+ Arp Schnitger, famous organmaker; some organs still playable
1719	Classical revival began
1722	"Six Brandenburg Concertos" composed by Bach
1725	Catherine the Great, Empress of Russia, promoted the arts
1740	English gardens, the great vogue
1740	Frederick the Great, King of Prussia, flute player, invited Bach
1750	+ Bach, at 65
1752	Ben Franklin's discoveries in electricity
1756	French and Indian War
1759	+ Handel, at 74

The Classical Period (1750-1820)

Music is to wash away the dust of every life.
—Dave Brubeck

If one word defines the Classical period it is simplicity. The Classical composers did away with the heaviness of the Baroque, the complex fugues and the opulent oratorios and operas. Three names dominate the music of the Classical period: Franz Joseph Haydn, Wolfgang Amadeus Mozart and Ludwig van Beethoven. Some have even designated them the First Viennese School, the second being of course the Twelve Tone School of Schoenberg.

The Baroque style had been going out of fashion for quite some time, as even Bach's sons referred to him as a great musician, but badly out of step. The transitional short-lived pre-classic period, designated as the Rococo in France and the Empfindsamer Stil in Germany, was already replacing the more pompous Baroque. Although a couple of respectable composers practiced this new style, Couperin, Loeillet, and the sons of Bach, especially C.P.E. Bach, soon became old-fashioned.

Partunient montes, nascetur ridiculus mus, so mused the poet Horace (65-8 B. C.). It may be translated as: "Mountains are in labor, the birth will be a ridiculous mouse." That may have been true for the Rococo style, but by about 1750 a new style was asserting itself more strongly, retiring the Baroque and the Rococo for good. The Classical period was the birth child this time.

Geniuses like Galileo and Newton had changed people's view of the world. Their great power of reasoning began undermining the authority of church and state. Voltaire and Diderot called it the "Age of Enlightenment," a turning point in history, daily life and especially the arts. Reason, not custom nor tradition, was the guiding-light. The middle class struggled for the same rights as the clergy and the aristocracy, thereby preparing the way for the American and French revolutions.

Revolutions now permeated politics, daily life and the arts. While artists like Watteau and Fragonard painted the rich and famous in pursuit of pleasure and fame, Jacques Louis David took part in the French Revolution, depicting heroism and patriotism with his allegorical paintings of ancient Rome. He was sending not so subtle a message to those in power.

Music also underwent a revolution. The new generation of composers was now free from the constraints of the Baroque music. While the Baroque had employed a single mood to a piece, the classical works toyed with diverse emotions—dramatic moments fluctuating with carefree, tuneful passages. Nevertheless great composers like Haydn, Mozart and Beethoven always maintained complete control, preserving unity with diversity.

The rhythm had been uniform and steady in the Baroque period; now the classical composers used sudden rhythmic changes, unexpected pauses, polyrhythms or bouncing syncopations. Melodic simplicity was the goal now and even the most profound works have a tune we can sing and remember.

Polyphonic textures were abandoned for melodies with simple harmonic background. The dynamic changes were sometimes so sudden and unexpected that they caused audiences to rise excitedly from their seats. The figured bass, the Baroque's musical shorthand, finally was dismissed and the faithful harpsichordist lost his job. The orchestra was enlarged, most instruments were paired and new instruments like trombones and clarinets added.

The Baroque composer had been happy with about twenty musicians; now orchestras of at least fifty, sometimes sixty members became common. The individual movements of the symphony often contrasted markedly, but in the end served the whole perfectly. The music becomes increasingly dramatic and passionate. And music was no longer for only the rich and famous but became the pursuit of the common man.

♪ Featured Music

Franz Joseph Haydn (1732-1809), *Surprise Symphony in G major* **(1791)**
Haydn was an Austrian composer. As a young boy he became one of the famous "Wiener Sängerknaben," Vienna Choirboys (still in existence). At 38 he took an orchestra post at the noble family Esterhazy estate and stayed there almost thirty years. After the death of his employer Haydn became a free-lancer, as many of his contemporaries had done. The first voyage he undertook was to London, where he knew Johann Salomon, who was a German-born violinist and impresario.

Haydn arrived on New Year's day 1791 in London. Once there he wrote several symphonies. He was so pleased with his success that he remained in London until June, 1792, thereby missing the funeral of his dear friend Mozart. This symphony is one of the second series of six such works. Its nickname "Surprise" stems from the loud drum beat at the conclusion of a soft beginning in the second movement. There are four variations on an original theme. These carefully crafted variations change the color, dynamics, rhythm, and melody and remain a favorite for today's audiences. Good music after a hard day's work!

W. A. Mozart (1756-91), *Symphony in g minor, fourth movement* **(1788)**
During the summer of 1788, in six weeks, Mozart wrote three symphonies at an incredible speed, while he continued numerous other works in progress. It is unclear why he composed these symphonies, and in such haste, but a commission must have been in the works. He never heard them performed because they were never sold. These symphonies, one even nicknamed the "Jupiter," are in strong contrast with one another like different personalities.

The first theme of the last movement of the g minor symphony is upsurging and highly dramatic, conveying a controlled feeling of tension. After an equally brusque bridge passage, the second theme is all smiles, using long smooth notes of relaxation. The development brings renewed tension, almost violent, with jagged downward leaps. Rapid shifts bring restless intensity. The greatest melodist of all the Classicists, Mozart here truly foreshadows the titanic Beethoven. These three symphonies are his last; he died within three years. These symphonies are Mozart's strongest utterances.

Ludwig van Beethoven (1770-1827), *Symphony #5, first movement* **(1808)**
Beethoven was born in Bonn; son and grandson of musicians. At 22 he left for Vienna ostensibly to study with Haydn. But he did not stay with Haydn, although stayed on in Vienna. He had many love-affairs, remember his Immortal Beloved, but he never married. The best known fact about his life is his struggle with deafness, which plagued him since his thirtieth year. He overcame this tragedy with only the greatest difficulty.

This is arguably the best known theme of any symphony, became even the Victory Theme of the Allies during WW II. This fateful opening dominates the entire work, permeating the first movement's every measure. Beethoven masterfully welds the entire movement into a coherent entity while enormously powerful with conflict and struggle. The second theme, generated from the first theme is calmer, while the rhythm of the first theme mutters in the low basses. In the development, with its ominous start, the second motive breaks into smaller and smaller fragments until only one single note survives. Then there is a breathtaking decrescendo with some forceful interruptions of the initial theme. The recapitulation rolls in the first theme with a thundering orchestra with a tremendous energy. Soon thereafter, instead of the customary repeat, a lost oboe sound is the sole survivor of the nightmare. The movement regains strength and ends with great power and unbridled force. The coda is so long it resembles a second, development. It is as if "Beethoven ist nicht ausgespielt," "Beethoven is not played out," not ready for the final chord, as when the coda enters everything is still in full swing. Only after a quasi "start over" that Beethoven abruptly ends the movement.

It is impossible to summarize Beethoven's art into one single piece. Beethoven began so many innovations, not only in enlarging the forms, but also in his very concise themes, overwhelming developments and the enormous emotional force mustered by his compositions. The first symphonies of Haydn employed only the instruments of the string quartet augmented with a double bass, two oboes and two horns. Later the Austrian master added two flutes, the bassoon, a trumpet and a pair of kettle-drums. Eventually the clarinet was added, especially beloved by Mozart. But Beethoven added trombones, and doubled all the instruments, added the contrabassoon, and a piccolo. For his Ninth symphony Beethoven had four horns, two trumpets, three trombones, triangle, cymbals and a large chorus! Obviously this was the beginning of the modem orchestra of a hundred players.

Jean Lesueur, a French composer and theorist, found the fifth symphony so exciting that he felt it shouldn't even exist! Luckily for us he never got his wish!

Characteristics of Classical Period Art and Music

C = Concise, sharp contrast from the preceding Baroque
L = Lucid, clear, precise, radiant, optimistic and carefree
A = Age of Enlightment, age of reason, age of elegance
S = Sonata-allegro form, fugues and the like abandoned
S = Sensitive and subtle
I = Intuitive, tuneful and simple
C = Contrast in dynamics, melody and rhythm (especially in the Sonata form)
A = Alternating between the dramatic and the carefree
L = Liberty through free-lance negotiations with patrons

Timeline 1750-1820

1746	Goya, Spanish painter of Royalty, + in Bordeau 1828, was against hypocrisy & cruelty
1748	Jacques Louis David born, French painter of revolutionary themes
1750	First concert hall

1750	Minuet popular dance in Europe
1754	First chocolate factory opened in Germany
1756	Pleyel built the first Grand Pianos in Paris
1764	+ William Hogarth, was 67, English painter of socially conscious satire
1764	Lead pencil invented by Faber (Germany)
1766	Guillotine invented in France
1769	Steam engine by James Watt—first steam engine powered car in Paris
1769	Smallpox vaccination by Dr. Edward Jenner of England
1770	Beginning of Industrial Revolution
1770	First public restaurants in Paris
1775	Age of Revolution
1776	War of the American Independence
1770-1790	Rococo Style (mostly in France and Germany)
1770	Beethoven born in Bonn, + 1827 in Vienna
1777	La Scala Opera House built in Milan
1778	Steel pens replace goose quills
1778	+ Rousseau was 66
1778	+ Voltaire was 84, wrote Candide in 1759
1778	Oboe invented in France
1780	Bifocals invented by Benjamin Franklin
1781	First hot air balloon in Paris—first parachute also in Paris
1781	Jean Houdon of France makes statues of Washington, Ben. Franklin, Jefferson
1782	Paganini, died in 1840. Great violin virtuoso.
1787	+ Gluck was 73, Bohemian composer, emigrated to Paris
1788	Mozart's "Marriage of Figaro" first performed in Prague
1788	Byron born, + in 1826
1789	George Washington elected first President of the U.S.
1789	French Revolution began
1790	Pencils invented
1791	+ Mozart, was 35
1791	Haydn in London, second time in 1794
1791	U.S.A. Bill of Rights
1792	Louvre becomes an art museum
1792	Gilbert Stuart paints George Washington
1792	Rossini, Italian composer of 36 operas, including Barber of Seville, died at 76
1795	Keats, + in 1821

1799	Rosetta stone found in Egypt, which made it possible to decipher hieroglyphics
1802	Victor Hugo writes his "Les Miserables"
1806	+ Fragonard was 76, French Rococo Style painter
1808	Napoleon in Spain, Portugal, Holland, Germany, Italy and Russia
1808	End of HOLY ROMAN EMPIRE through Napoleon's campaign
1808	Popular dances in U.S.: polka, Mazurka and quadrille
1808	Daumier + 1879, French caricature painter of everyday life
1808	Beethoven's Fifth Symphony
1808	Carl Maria von Weber, a German, wrote the first "Romantic" opera, Oberon
1808	Goethe's Faust finished
1809	+ Thomas Paine, American revolutionary
1809	+ Haydn at 77
1811	Metronome invented by Johann Maezel in Vienna
1812	Napoleon in Moscow with 600,000 (lost over 500,000 men)
1815	Battle of Waterloo
1821	Der Freischutz, Carl Maria Von Weber, first truly Romantic opera
1822	Bolshoi Ballet Company founded in Moscow
1827	+ Beethoven at 56
1828	+ Schubert at 31

The Romantic Period (1820-1910)

*Beauty in music is too often confused with something
that lets the ear lie back in an easy chair.*
—Charles Ives

Separating the Classical from the Romantic era is difficult, but possible, since there is a definite break between the two eras. The difference is actually enormous. We can sense it just by listening to Berlioz' Symphonie Fantastique and Beethoven's Ninth Symphony. In fact only 5 years separates the two pieces. No matter how unbuttoned Beethoven becomes, he always controls the form, harmonies and orchestration. Nevertheless Beethoven pushed the expressive envelope to the next level—music as self-expression. That is one reason why Beethoven, more than any composer, dominates the music even up to today. And yet Berlioz managed to push that same envelope yet farther out.

Emotion, imagination, and individualism were the primary Romantic goals. Freedom of expression was everyone's password, with subjectivity as its companion. The Industrial Revolution gave rise to a capitalistic, wealthy class. For the first time ever, the artists and the composers had large audiences for whom they could work and perform, among them potential patrons with increasing wealth. Meanwhile, artists, no longer beholden to anyone, became commonplace. Concert managers, business agents and music critics all promoted a strong motivation for music fitting the masses. The newly established academies and conservatories for teaching of the arts and music promoted a high degree of proficiency and knowledge. Symphonic music, opera and the ballet, all accelerated.

Walt Whitman wrote, "I celebrate myself, and sing myself." William Wordsworth echoed "All good poetry is the spontaneous overflow of powerful feelings." Exploring their inner self the romantics were drawn to the fantasy, the unconscious, the irrational, the world of dreams and the macabre. Even the titles of their books are evidence of this world, such as The Cask of Amontillado by Edgar Allen Poe; Frankenstein by Mary Wollstonecraft Shelley; the Confessions of an English Opium-Eater by Thomas De Quincey. This spirit of madness extended from music to literature and to the visual arts. The latter was exemplified by Goya's famous "black paintings" of demons, ghouls and man-eating monsters, whose meaning is still very obscure. Eugene Delacroix, the noted painter of Chopin's portrait, also withdraws to the mysterious and depicted violent scenes in exotic lands. He completely rejected neoclassicism, preferring distorted forms and dramatic coloring to express the action-packed scenes of foreign lands.

Writers waxed enthusiastically about the Medieval era, with its chivalry and romance, besides musing over landscape and nature. The delights of the effete, decadent salons moved the artists to the forests and the hillside, to dream their private reveries, delving into introspection and contemplation with overwhelming heart. A most gripping novel is Les Miserables by Victor Hugo; "it is the march from evil to good, from injustice to justice, from the false to the true.... from rottenness to life, from brutality to duty, from Hell to Heaven, from nothingness to God" as he writes in his dedication. It is the story of the Parisian underworld and the barricades of the uprising of 1832. It is about the persecution of Valjean, imprisoned for stealing a loaf of bread, but the bitter and relentless Inspector Javert; the desperation of the prostitute Fantine; the bittersweet love between the rebel Marius and the young Cosette; the vicious amorality of the rogue Thenardier; and the heroic battle between the forces of democracy and tyranny.

The Age of Reason evolved to the Age of Feelings. No wonder today there is a renewed craving for that era, as nowadays, the romantic drive towards a harmonic integration of humanity and nature had fresh appeal in our world wherein individuals seem increasingly devalued.

In the visual arts landscape painting was no longer a decorative background for the Romantic artists, but a poetic and respectable subject. William Turner (1775-1851) that great English painter of the blazing Houses of Parliament consumed by fire, celebrated nature's sublime elemental forces, and man's futile struggle against them. Turner's great technical facility enabled him to suggest as much as he actually showed. His work is full of storms, wind, fire, mist and water, and imparts breathtaking dazzling effects even on the most indifferent onlooker.

The previously mentioned Berlioz was most responsible for a seachange in the music. He used varied instrumental possibilities to express the emotional currents within his Symphony Fantastique. Many of his other pieces, especially his Requiem, unleashed enormous powers. Its performance on 5 December 1837 was more gripping than any brimstone preaching! The priests at the altar wept openly and ambulances were summoned for those people overcome by the deafening, ominous power of 16 kettledrums, 600 singers, four brass bands, and a 300 strong orchestra, at the famous Dies Irae—Day of Wrath. Berlioz in his Memoirs writes with passion about his music, but of his Requiem he says "If I were threatened with seeing my entire oevre burned, less one score, it would be for the Messe des morts that I would beg mercy."

The piano rapidly replaced the antiquated harpsichord and soon became a household item. The piano matched the full orchestra's extreme range of sound, creating volume while even able to sustain pitches. Most composers of that era wrote for the instrument, most notably Schubert, Schumann, Chopin, Liszt, Brahms and Rachmaninov.

During the Romantic era, there was a close interrelationship among the arts. This fusion of all the arts contributed not only to Wagner's "Gesammtkunst" (integrated art) vision in the opera, but also in other artistic expressions. Franz Schubert was enchanted by Schiller's poetry; Delacroix' paintings were inspired by the romantic poetry of Byron and Goethe.

Realism also was part of romanticism. Charles Dickens and Emile Zola wrote about the brutal lives of the working class and George Bizet's Carmen, tells the story of a cigarette factory worker, Carmen, and the amorous toreador, Escamillo, in conflict with the jealous Don Jose. Although said by Beethoven, the last of the

Classicists, "music comes from the heart and goes back to the heart" Beethoven's battle cry became the battle cry of the Romanticists as well.

♪ Featured Music

Hector Berlioz (1803-69), *Symphonic Fantastique, fourth and fifth movement* **(1830)** This French Composer had general music training at the Paris Conservatory, although he was not proficient on any instrument. He was a great innovator, not only in musical content, but also in orchestration.

While in Paris to study medicine, he fell in love with Harriet Smithson, an English actress. Since she ignored him, he wrote this symphony to attract her attention. Though eventually they married, he soon abandoned her.

He was more accepted in Germany than in his own country and he died rather disillusioned. Although his repertoire is immense and grandiose, he was rebuffed continually in Paris. Increasingly bitter, his energies spent, Berlioz did not compose during the last seven years of his life.

Most of his symphonies do not need a script, especially not one written in advance. It reads like an autobiography, but in fact, it is not.

Here is the script: A young musician of morbidly sensitive sensibilities and fiery temperament has taken a narcotic, too weak to kill him, plunging him into a deep slumber accompanied by the strangest visions, during which his sensations, emotions, and memories are transformed in his sick mind into musical thoughts and images. The beloved one has become a melody to him, an idee fixe ("fixed idea") as it were, that he encounters and hears everywhere, especially when he sees or thinks of her. (The idee fixe will later become a musical device in operas and even movies.)

IV.   March to the Scaffold: He dreams that after he kills his beloved, he is condemned to death and led to the scaffold. The procession moves forward to the sounds of a march that is alternatively somber and fierce, then brilliant and solemn. Muffled sounds of heavy steps change suddenly to the noisiest clamor. Towards the end, the idee fixe returns for a moment, like a last thought of love interrupted by the fatal blow of the guillotine. The crowds applaud. All are realistically portrayed in the music.

V.   Death of the Witches' Sabbath: He sees himself at the Sabbath, in the midst of ghosts, sorcerers, monsters, and ghouls, gathered for his funeral. Strange noises, groans, bursts of laughter, and distant cries are heard. The beloved

"Idee fixe" theme appears again, but it has lost its character of nobility and shyness. It has become no more than a dance tune—mean, trivial, and grotesque: Is she coming to join the Sabbath? A joyous roar announces her arrival, and later takes part in the devilish orgy. It's all there—funeral bells, a burlesque parody on the Dies Irae, in a wild round-dance.

Berlioz devised many unusual blends in the orchestra; he demanded many unconventional sounds from the instruments, and always had a full array of percussion instruments for different effects. He wanted 240 strings, thirty harps, thirty pianos, and at least a dozen kettle drums. It is unclear if he ever realized those enormous proportions. The first performance was a disaster as there were not enough chairs and music stands for such a large mob of performers.

Robert Schumann (1810-56) *Auf-Schwung (Searing)* **from the** *Fantasiestucke*
Schumann had to abandon his intended career as virtuoso pianist because of hand injuries brought on by a mechanical device for finger-development. Perhaps this was Carpel Tunnel Syndrome. He married his teacher's daughter, Clara Wieck, in 1840—she was then 21, and a concert pianist and composer in her own right. In 1854 he threw himself into the Rhine after developing mental instability. He died in a mental institution two years later. He was a superb songwriter and piano composer of the highest order. During the first ten years of his creative output, Schumann published only piano pieces. But at Clara's urging, after 1840, Schumann turned to symphonies and chamber music. She said that he had found the sphere for which his great imagination fitted him. He eventually wrote four symphonies, although his best work still lies with works for the piano and the voice.

Frederic Chopin (1810-49), *Polonaise in A,* **surnamed** *The Military* **(1838)**
Chopin, born in Warsaw, Poland, is known as the "poet of the piano, as he is the only great composer who wrote exclusively for this instrument. His companion, the famous novelist George Sand, left a memorable account of Chopin at work:

> *His creative power was spontaneous, miraculous. It came to him without effort or warming... But then began the most heartrending labor I have ever witnessed. It was a series of attempts, of fits of resolution and impatience to recover certain details. He would shut himself in his room for days, pacing up and down, breaking his pens, repeating and modifying one bar a hundred times.*

Chopin died of tuberculosis in Paris at the age of thirty-nine. The artistic world bid him farewell to the strains of his own funeral march, from his B-flat minor piano sonata.

The heroic side of Chopin shows itself in the most popular of his Polonaises, written in the ternary form, ABA. In the B section the emotional temperature drops considerably, as it is time to sing out a memorable melody sustained by the initial rhythm of the beginning. Essential to Chopin's style is the tempo rubato—a difficult term to describe, except to say that the tempo fluctuates, without upsetting the basic beat. Rubato, used sparingly like any seasoning, is most effective and almost inherent to the music of Chopin. Born in Poland to a French father, Chopin is considered Poland's national composer. He arrived in Paris at the age of twenty-one, never returning to his native Warsaw. His friends included the poet Heinrich Heine, the painter Eugene Delacroix, the novelists Victor Hugo, George Sand and Alexandre Dumas and the composers Liszt and Berlioz. Although Chopin was influenced by the intellectuals of France, his heart always remained in Poland.

Richard Strauss (1864-1949), *Till Eulenspiegel's Merry Pranks* **(1895)**
Richard Strauss was born in Munich and later settled in Garmish Partenkirchen, the famous town of the Passion play. He always boasted of being no relation to the Waltz kings of Vienna. Strauss, born into a musical family, achieved fame while still in his early twenties, with some spectacular tone-poems. Then he turned to the opera in which he equally excelled. His best work was written before 1910, especially "Don Juan," "Also sprach Zarathustra" "Tod und Verklarung" and of course "Till Eulenspiegel." The most famous operas are "Salome," "Electra" and the electrifying comedy the "Rosenkavalier." His music is indebted to Wagner, always heavy and serious, dramatic and nervous. Strauss is one of the last Romantic composers, who overlived the style by half a century!

Strauss himself added the annotation—"in rondo form." *Till Eulenspiegel* the old-fashioned rogue of Medieval German folklore is not unlike our own "Dennis the Menace." The composer did not provide a detailed account of all the mischievous frolicking, but no imagination is needed to see Till jump on his horse, overturning the stands on the market, while the merchants run and shriek. Disguised as a priest, he preaches morals while out of his toe peeps the rascal. As a cavalier he falls in love, first in jest, then in earnest, then being rebuffed, he curses all mankind. Soon he forgets that too, and mockingly argues with some learned professors. One day he pushes too far, is tried in court and while whistling defiantly, ascends the gallows to be hung. Till is dead. But his music reappears, he is back and new adventures are about to begin.

Franz Liszt (1811-1886), *Totentanz* (began in 1849)

Franz List was Hungarian by birth, but in fact was always more of a cosmopolitan. He lived in Paris, Switzerland, Italy, and Germany. Although he never married he was always entertaining illicit love affairs. While in Weimar, before the center of poetry under Goethe, now under Liszt's leadership, became the focal point of modern music.

During a visit to Pisa, Franz Liszt was attracted to the painting—the Triumph of Death—a vivid representation of the Black Death of 1350. The tense, even diabolic, feeling of the Dies Irae, with dazzling virtuoso passages is pushed almost to the edge of terror. The Fantasy opens with a brutal hammering of the theme setting the stage for the awesome meaning of the "Dies Irae," Day of wrath. A dazzling set of variations.

Listz was the first composer who was also a great performer. Brilliant, passionate, and poetic, he was one of the era's finest virtuosos. His music at times is bombastic and trivial but came from a real extroverted Romantic original. He found new ways to exploit the piano, which was almost like his private orchestra, demanding the enormous range of the very soft to the thunderously loud. He requires enormous physical strength at octave playing, while in the next measures exacting rapid passages and wide leaps. Liszt had hopes of marrying the Princess Caroline von Sayn-Wittgenstein, but the Pope exercised his veto, because her husband was still living. In 1861 Liszt abruptly began studying theology in Rome and soon became Abbé Liszt, to the astonishment of his contemporaries. He had been known as an incorrigible Don Juan, having Herculean powers at the piano. Now he wrote organ music, oratorios and masses, feeling a mission to reform and renew the church music! Except for the tone poem "Les Préludes" and his piano concertos his work is now largely neglected, especially his oratorios and other church music.

Richard Wagner (1813-1883), *Ride of the Valkeries* (1856)

Born in Leipzig, more than likely illegitimate, his true father eventually married his mother. He soon was swept up in the opera, but detected its pitfalls early on. Being sued several times for financial improprieties he fled to Paris. Later on he worked in Dresden. There he joined some revolutionaries and fled to Weimar, where Liszt was his protector. An amnesty restored his citizenship to his Fatherland! In 1863 King Ludwig, named "mad King Ludwig," the one who built Neuschwanstein's fairy castle, financed Wagner's every desire and made his "Ring" a possibility. It was his masterpiece. Wagner was meanwhile living with Cosima Liszt, the daughter of the composer and wife to the famous conductor

Hans von Bülow. Only after the death of Wagner's wife, Minna Planer, and her divorce would he marry Cosima. Wagner's life reads like a novel!

Nietzsche was initially a wild admirer of Wagner's music, but later on heckled him with sarcastic terms in his anti-semitic writings.

Wagner was always dreaming and in 1872 his ultimate dream was made possible with the building of the Festspielhaus in Bayreuth, and he promptly composed "Parsifal" for its exclusive use. But all this titanic work eventually took its toll and Wagner died exhausted in Venice. He left an indelible mark on the music and his influence was felt until the advent of 20th century music.

The dramatic prelude to the third act of "Die Walküre," the first of the quatrology of the "Ring der Nibelungen," portrays an oncoming storm, while a strong rhythmic figure stimulates the Valkeries' horses galloping through the night.

"For most of the audiences the Ride of the Valkeries doesn't describe Nordic warrior-maidens on horseback taking slain heroes to their eternal rest in Valhalla—it describes helicopters attacking a Vietnamese village village," notes filmmaker Francis Ford Coppola, who used the music successfully in Apocalypse Now.

Wagner called his operas, "music dramas," emphasizing the interrelationship between drama and music. Opera, of course, had always been a fusion of all the arts, but Wagner emphasized it even more strongly than before. He always talked about his integrated art, Gesamtkunst.

His life, escapades and romances reads like the best of fictionalized espionage novels of a profoundly selfish, ruthless, and self-important musical genius. Even the characters in his music dramas were heroes, gods and demigods. All of his librettos, which he wrote himself, were based on medieval Germanic legends, music and spectacle.

Guiseppe Verdi (1813-1901), *La donna e mobile, from Rigoletto, third act* **(1851)**
Verdi is the quintessential Italian and Wagner's worthy counterpart. Wagner wrote essentially for the German elite, while Verdi wrote for the ordinary people whose main entertainment was opera. Wagner's music is based on highly philosophical subjects, while Verdi is preoccupied with the drama of daily life. Wagner's music is hardly singable or understandable by the average listener, as Verdi's music has a distinct folksy slant to it and even vendors would whistle his tunes while delivering their goods. "Of all styles, the boring style is the worst" he said.

Verdi wanted his operas to be "original, interesting, and passionate...passionate above all." Verdi was highly venerated and became a national hero. Even before Rigoletto's premiere, Verdi knew that his catchy tune would be a hit and literally hid the music from all involved. He wanted it to remain a surprise!

Verdi was born to a family of poor farmers near Parma, but always was proud to be a farmer! He was a rather shy man, who shunned the limelight cast on him. Eventually he became a national icon and his very name the motto of freedom. VERDI = Vittore Emmanuele, Re D'Italia. Victor Emmanuel, King of Italy, became the battle cry to reinstall the monarchy in Italy and shed the tyranny of Austria and France. The list of operas is endless: Rigoletto, Il Travatore, La Traviata, Aida and his last two, Otello and Falstaff, the latter written when he was in his eighties! But his greatest "opera" is his Requiem, written in 1874 in memory of his friend, the poet Manzoni. Although Verdi adapted some of Wagner's ideas of integrating the story with the arias, nevertheless he stays miles away from Wagner. Never will he abandon the sensual singability of his easy melodies in favor of the orchestra. His art is essentially for the simple folks, his neighbors.

Nationalism in Nineteenth-Century Music

1848 was the year of the failed revolutions: on February 24, Paris, against King Louis Philippe; March 1, Vienna, against the Hapsburg's government of Metternich; March 3, Hungary; March 15, Berlin; March 18, Bohemia; March, 18, Milan, then eventually it was the turn of Venice, Tuscany, Sardinia, etc. All these revolutions stunned but did not break the old regimes. Indeed by September of the same year all the revolutions had been crushed.

In the arts, however, revolutions were far more successful in asserting new artistic independence, especially the distancing from the Austrian/German ideal. Chopin, Liszt, Dvorak, and Smetana stirred strong emotions at home and left lasting ethnic impressions abroad. It is also the time when five Russians formed an alliance called the "Mighty Handful": Mussorgsky, Rimsky-Korsakov, Balakirev, Borodin and Cui took up a consciously "nationalistic" standpoint in music, drawing much upon Russian folklore, history and literature.

Russia and the Balkan countries' culture and music made the nationalistic trends obvious. But other countries also had ardent composers using their own folk songs and legends to inspire their music. Ralph Vaughan Williams in England, Manuel de Falla in Spain, Jean Sibelius in Finland, Edvard Grieg in Norway and Ottorina Respighi in Italy all had a passion for their native country.

Soon Brahms became enamored with the gypsies' violin playing and employed their techniques into his violin concerto and his now famous Hungarian Rhapsodies. In France composers like Bizet poured into their work, especially the opera "Carmen" a strong dose of Spanish ethnic music. But the Nationalists wanted even more than imitating others' music; they rather promoted their own music, not built on abstract models, but with a strong folk music input. Nietzsche, who had become disenchanted with Wagner's pathos urged the composers to "mediterranize" the music, implying thereby strongly to de-Germanize the music. Folk music was a new source of inspiration and human pride. The nationalistic tendency is still present; Debussy, who called himself "musicien Français," and also the early pieces of Stravinsky, have a strong nationalistic feel.

Bedrich Smetana (1824-1884), *The Moldau (Ma Vlast)* **(1874)**
Smetana was the first to write an opera about and in the mother tongue of his native country, Bohemia, freed from the Austrians in 1848. He took part in the unsuccessful struggle against Austria and emigrated to Sweden for about twelve years to avoid reprisal. At fifty, though becoming suddenly deaf, he wrote six symphonic poems glorifying Bohemia's history and legends. His deafness was a source of great trial and he dealt with it less well than Beethoven before him. Smetana wrote the following program to preface his score:

> *The composition depicts the river, beginning from its two small sources, one cold the other warm, the joining of both streams into one, then the flow of the Moldau through forests and across meadows, through the countryside where merry beasts are celebrated; water nymphs dance in the moonlight; on the nearby rocks can be seen the outline of ruined castles, proudly soaring into the sky. The Moldau swirls through the St. Johns Rapids and flows in a broad stream toward Prague. It passes Vysehrad, and finally the river in the distance as it flows majestically into the Elbe.*

Smetana follows this to the letter. The folk-like theme represents the river. The work is at once calm and turbulent, in unison with the politics of his country. The piece starts with the two sources of the river, gradually introducing the famous river theme. Then the river flows through a hunting forest and past a village in which a wedding celebration takes place. After a calmer night, the river greets the new day with the river theme, and after some turbulence at the St. John Rapids, the river approaches the big city: Prague, the capital, city with a past and a future, city in which the Renaissance composer Philip de Monte found an audience, where the German Hassler was happy and where Mozart always was eagerly awaited. With this work Smetana proved his skill as a composer of program music, and also his love for his country.

Antonin Dvorak (1841-1904), *Symphony #9, New World Symphony* **(1893)**
Dvorak followed Smetana as the leading composer of Czech national music. But while Smetana was attracted to program music, Dvorak only wrote absolute music. Nevertheless he uses rhythms (polka, furiant, dumka etc.) inherent to the Bohemian people. When Dvorak was about thirty-six, his fame spread rapidly, aided by Brahms, who had recommended him to his publisher.

In 1892 he came to New York for three years as director of the National Conservatory. Dvorak encouraged his students to write American music, by incorporating native themes and African-American spirituals, and embracing "the fine music growing up from her own soil and having its own character—the natural voice of a free and great nation."

His symphony is permeated with spirituals. In the first movement the first theme begins in minor with a syncopated figure that dominates the entire symphony. The second theme is a gentle dance and a third theme is drawn from "Swing Low, Sweet Chariot." In his development Dvorak concentrates on the first and third themes, which he combines and constantly varies. The coda brings the first movement to a powerful and climatic conclusion.

The second movement is a deep felt melody, and although build from "Going home," an American homegrown spiritual, has a profound nostalgic quality heightened by the nasal sound of the English horn.

The Third movement is all in the spirit of the dance and the last movement reintroduces some of the themes of the previous movements and he ends the symphony with a passionate and triumphant summary.

Although Dvorak left the States after only three years, this symphony is a worthy souvenir of his stay and work here.

Jean Sibelius (1865-1957), *Finlandia* **(1899)**
Sibelius is Finland's glory. He studied in Berlin and Vienna, but remained faithful to his Finnish heritage. Much of his music had Finnish roots, sometimes relating to the "Kalevala," a Finnish national epic poem. A government grant enabled him to give up teaching and devote himself to composing, although he did not publish anything after 1926!

Sibelius wrote this music while Finland was still oppressed under the iron rule of the Russian Czars. The work was considered so provocative that its performance was forbidden. When Finland achieved independence in December 1917, Finlandia symbolized triumph and freedom.

After a brooding introduction, the first theme has a sweeping melody with up-lifting rhythm that eventually merges into the hymn-like second theme. The music has all the outward features of a folk song, although the tunes are Sibelius' own.

Sibelius' best work is a reflection of the Finnish landscape, icy and forbidding, full of sobering melancholy while a dreamlike hazy expression fills the soul of the listener. In spite of some longwinded passages Sibelius knows how to keep the form under control. His music carried his name far beyond the borders of his native country.

Ralph Vaughan Williams (1872-1958), *Fantasia on Greensleeves* **(1929)**
Vaughan Williams is an English composer through and through. And even though he studied abroad with Max Bruch and Ravel, his language has remained essentially English and Romantic. Because of his deep love for the English folk music, some of which he collected and arranged, he can easily be placed with the nationalists of that period. Because of the English folk song, his music has a distinct modal quality mostly interwoven with free-flowing contrapuntal combinations, oblivious of the harmonic consequences. This new approach to the treasure of folk music is refreshing and lifts it from the dusty cupboards to the level of great art. Although most of his music has a formal packaging, like symphonies, variations, overtures, fantasias all speak of things English. His music also has a strong undercurrent of mysticism, perhaps innate, since he grew up in a parsonage. Because of this influence he wrote much church music of high quality.

The Fantasia on Greensleeves is typical Vaughan Williams. It was first introduced in his Shakespearian opera "Sir John in Love." This is a beautiful arrangement of two folk songs: one Greensleeves, allegedly by Henry the VIII, and the other tune "Lovely Joan." Is it the name of Sir John's love? Very subtle variation technique is employed, beautifully clothed in an array of strings, flute and harp.

Manuel de Falla (1876-1946), *El Amor brujo* **(1915)**
De Falla was born in exotic Cadiz. From 1907 to 1914 he mingled in the circles frequented by Debussy, Dukas and Ravel in Paris and soon became a world figure in his own right. Although living for seven years in France, his music never lost its original passion and fiery fervor for his native Spain nor was it diluted with the sweet wine of the French cuisine.

Manuel de Falla was a rather retiring, ascetic person who wrote fewer and fewer pieces, while shrinking his instrumentation to chamber orchestra proportions. Some of his later work does not use folk melodies at all, but he extracted the essential characteristics of the Spanish idiom: the conflicting rhythms of the castanets, the sonorities of the guitar, and Moorish influence in their melodies. He expresses with passionate sincerity the soul of the sun-bleached, barren landscape of Spain.

De Falla was never a very prolific composer but every piece is a masterwork. In 1940 he left for Argentina and retired to the house of his sister at Alta Gracia, working on "Atlanta" which was to remain unfinished.

The subtitle to the ballet "El amor brujo" is "Gypsy scene from Andalusia." Without actually quoting examples of Andalusian music, de Falla evoked an impression of gypsy music, even adding their typical mode of singing. In this one-act drama of love and jealousy, the ghost of the dead lover of the hot-blooded gypsy returns to frustrate her new love affair. She cunningly contrives to exorcise the ghost and salvages her relationship with her true love. The climax of the ballet is the Ritual Fire Dance performed at midnight after the twelve strokes of midnight. De Falla portrays his Spain as fiery, passionate and essentially dominated by love, jealousy and mystical forces.

Ottorino Respighi (1879-1936), *Pines of Rome* (1926)
Respighi was born in Bologna, Italy, a city with a long academic and musical tradition. His two visits to Russia between 1900 and 1903, lessons from Rimsky-Korsakov and Richard Strauss the French "impressionists" definitely had a beneficial effect on his deft manipulation of is orchestration. During his formative years he was very active as a pianist and string player, and started to cultivate a love for some old Italian music that had been neglected. Most delightful are his "Ancient Airs and Dances." As of 1913 he settled in Rome. His greatest promoter was Toscanini, who catapulted him into a world figure.

His "Pines of Rome" and the "Fountains of Rome," both are considered his best work. Not only the musical substance, but especially his masterful orchestration, lush, eclectic, colorful, are most noteworthy. He had been a student of Rimsky after all! The Pines of Rome starts with children at play in the Villa Borghese, while suddenly they are attracted to the catacombs nearby, whence come the plaintive sounds of Gregorian chant. Then comes nightfall over the Janiculum complete with a gramophonic(!) nightingale. The dawn breaks over the Appian Way, the ancient road of the Romans to the south of their empire. An army is marching in lockstep to a relentless and obstinate rhythm set by the lower instruments. A most impressive work and a superb commentary and tour guide to the sight and sounds of Rome.

Characteristics of Romantic art and Music

R = Range of emotion greatly expanded
0 = Orchestra enlarge in all sections, especially brass and percussion
M = Medieval and Ancient art revered
A = Art for Art's sakes—music beyond entertainment, art carries a statement
N = Nationalism emphasized
T = Most works have titles (including the paintings)
I = Illusion, fantasy, and the exotic are predominant.
C = Continuing impact on today's audiences.
I = Influences of Shakespeare, Goethe, Rembrandt and Beethoven
S = Subjectivity with strong individualism
M = Music and all the other arts have a powerful message

Timeline from 1820 to 1900

1809	Edgar Allen Poe (+ 1849)
1810	U.S. Population 7,300,000 - slaves 1,200,000
1811	Metronome invented by Maelzel, Vienna
1814	Francis Scott Key writes "The Star-Spangled Banner"
1815	Goya's "Witches' Sabbath," most obscure painting!
1818	Karl Marx + 1883
1818	Silent Night composed (Franz Gruber) as well as Ave Maria by Schubert
1820	Shelley's "Prometheus unbound"
1822	Bolshoi Ballet Co. founded in Moscow
1825	Invention of the rain in England—soon introduced in the U. S.
1826	Beginning of photography—color photos in 1882
1826	Goethe writes "Faust"
1826	+ Jefferson, + Adams
1826	Stephen Foster (+64) composer of many popular songs, dies at 38.
1827	The accordion invented in Vienna—first upright piano built in England
1832	Telegraph invented
1835	Hans Christian Andersen starts writing his 168 children's stories
1835	The Grimm brothers write Snow White, Cinderella, Hansel & Gretel
1837	Victoria, Queen of England for 64 years, Empress of India in 1877

1839	First steam ships
1839	Edgar Allan Poe writes the Raven, The Gold Bug, The Pit and the Pendulum
1840	Morse code invented
1840	Monet, impressionistic painter (+ 1926)
1841	Emerson's Essays.
1842	The New York Philharmonic, America's first symphony orchestra
1845	Stephen Foster wrote Swanee River, Camptown Races, etc.
1848	The Communist Manifest; Workers Unite Against Capitalism
1846	Potato famine in Ireland—over 100,000 migrated to the U. S.
1848	Revolutions in France, Germany, Austria, Hungary, Romania, Ireland, Italy, etc.
1849	Goldrush in the Western U. S.
1851	The temperate scale universally adopted (octave = 12 equal semi-tones)
1852	Harriet Beecher Stowe's Uncle Tom's Cabin
1853	The Henry Steinway Piano Company opened in New York City
1853	Vincent Van Gogh, post-impressionistic painter (+ 1890)
1854	Crimean war, where Florence Nightingale distinguished herself
1855	Invention of mass manufacture of steel
1857	Beginning of Free Libraries
1859	Darwin's Origin of Species
1859	World's first oil well in Titusville, PA
1860	Italy unified
1861-1865	Civil War in U. S.
1861	Italy becomes a kingdom—Victor Emmanuel king
1862	Victor Hugo's Les Miserables
1865	Tolstoy's War and Peace novel based on the uprising of 1832 in Paris
1866	Use of dynamite
1867	Cro-Magnon man discovered in France
1868	Impressionist movement starts with Monet, Renoir and Pissaro
1869	Henri Matisse (+ 1954)
1870	Franco-Prussian War (France lost and paid heavy indemnity)
1871	Phonograph invented by Thomas Edison
1872	The first National Park in Yellowstone opened
1875	Cave paintings from 13,000 B. C. discovered in Altamira, Spain
1876	Combustion engine will lead to the invention of the automobile in 1885)
1877	Microphone invented, will eventually affect music profoundly

1879	after more than 10,000 experiments Edison invents the light bulb
1880	Scramble for the partition of Africa. (Most European countries involved)
1881	Pablo Picasso (+ 1973)
1883	Nietzsche's "Thus Spake Zarathustra"
1886	Statue of Liberty, gift from France
1886	Daimler invents the gasoline powered motor
1889	Eiffel Tower completed; monster or new landmark?
1893	"America the Beautiful" composed by Samuel Ward
1894	Diesel engine
1894	Nicolas II, last Czar of Russia crowned
1895	X-rays
1895	Movie projector invented by Thomas Edison
1895	Marconi invents the radio
1899	Interpretation of dreams by Freud
1899	Maple Leaf Rag written by Scott Joplin (1868-1917)

Impressionism

When all the muses come together they dance.
—Edgar Degas

If one word personifies Impressionism it must be a French word, something along the lines of: delicate, exquisite, charming, but Impressionism is yet much more than those adjectives, as appropriate as they are. Impressionism began at the dawn of the twentieth century, a seed-time for far-reaching changes in the arts, science and technology and just about every aspect of the human condition.

Although the word Impression was first used to deride Monet's Sunrise (1874), it soon became the banner for all late-romantic painters in France. The history books settle on 1874 as the formal launch of the movement. That year most of the artists—among them Monet, Pissaro, Degas, Renoir, Sisley and Moisot—borrowed a large empty space for a joint show in Paris. With a few exceptions, the critics hated it; one of them had lifted the word from a Monet title, dismissively using the word "impression" in his review. Although it had come up before, it would now become a formal label. This word, this concept does not begin to encompass the radical changes fostered by the new, modem art. Their representations suggested rather than defined outlines, details and forms. Until now art was always largely expected to please the eye. Looking back, historians would acknowledge that the event marked the end of an era and the dawn of modern art.

Literature also came under the spell of the so-called "fin de siècle" (end of the century)—an ambiguous term as much as malaise (uneasiness), the other over-used word of that time. These avant-garde poets and writers ripped away the veils of complacency, setting out to demolish the façade of bygone years. Impression was more important than form and meaning, addressing more the senses than the intellect. Foremost of these symbolist poets of the Impressionist era were Paul Verlaine, Stéfane Mallarmé, and Arthur Rimbaud. Verlaine said it all in one gulp:

> *For we desire above all—nuance,*
> *Not color but half-shades!*
> *Ah! Nuance alone unites*
> *Dream with dream and flute with horn.*

As usual Paris was the center of all French activity. Paris' influence and theories infused the other half of the world, and although in essence inherently French, composers and artists from other countries, especially Americans studying in Paris, came to write and paint in that fascinating style.

Baudelaire, the great French poet of that time, wrote:

> *La tout n'est qu'ordre et beauté*
> *Luxe, calme at volupté.*

"Here is only order and beauty, luxury, calmness and ecstasy," the interpretation of the delicate, sensuous play of the sophisticated dreams and longings.

In music, Impressionism somehow came when it was needed to replace the over-blown, over-saturated Romantic era. The major-minor system that had served so well for the last three hundred years began to feel its limitations. Newer scales, (actually Greek scales and church modes from the Middle Ages) were introduced that gave their music an archaic, novel slant. Primitive pentatonic scales (five whole step scales) were revived, as well as some coming from other non-Western music: the Moorish strains emanating from Spain or the gamelan sounds from the Javanese orchestras as heard during the World Exposition of 1889. The gamelan is a highly sophisticated orchestra with various types of chimes, gongs, xylophones, two-stringed violins, flutes and a whole array of drums and other percussive instruments—this was to greatly influence the "new music." All these imports and the American jazz rhythms offered a bewitching contrast to the traditional music of the late-romantics. Rhythms were completely overhauled and the impressionistic composers replaced the traditional strong first beat accent with a fluid, gliding way of floating rhythms. Besides the great innovations of melody, rhythm, and harmony was the newly subtly colored palette of the orchestra. The Impressionists shunned the lush, booming sonority of the Romantic, i.e. German orchestra, for the veiled blending of shimmering colors, the unusual timbres of the low register of the flute and clarinet, the discreetly muted brass, and the lustrous upper range of the violins topped with a silvery gossamer glockenspiel or the tingling of the triangle.

A great master in this innovation was unquestionably Debussy—a goldsmith working with the delicate colors of precious stones. Even the titles of the Impressionistic works, more suggestions than stories, give it all away; Poissons rouges (goldfish), Nuages (clouds), La mer (the sea), all highly atmospheric.

What is most interesting is that Monet and Debussy, who we commonly associate with Impressionism, vigorously denied the "Impressionist" label put on them. Monet's friends were sent a mock funeral announcement on January 24, 1880, in anticipation of Monet's withdrawal from the Impressionist circle, this on behalf of Degas, Cassatt, Caillebotte, Pissaro, his ex-friends, ex-students and ex-supporters.

That's how angry they were at his distancing himself from the movement. And yet, Monet is the artist who has made the most innovative contributions to landscape painting, by insisting to be in the fields, his face burnt by the blazing sun or his hands frozen by the cruel winter-wind.

Debussy also disliked being lumped together with the "Impressionists." He wrote to his publisher Durand in 1908, concerning his orchestral piece "Images pour orchestre": "I am trying to make something new—realities, as it were: what imbeciles call 'Impressionism.'" Sounds like a contemptuous denouncement to anyone reading this. Implying therefore that Debussy ever considered finding a musical parallel to the moods and intent of the impressionistic painters is misleading.

Although most of the impressionistic arts are very much in tune with nature, nevertheless there is a strong reaction against naturalism. Their poetic souls strive against the domination of the machine, the cold-calculated scientific analysis and the deadening materialistic philosophies. Being slave to the realistic rendition of their surroundings is completely counter to their own concept of life. The artists and intellectuals claim once more their unrestricted right and are probing the depths of the soul.

There, in the soul, they find a beauty that their eyes can't see: the wonders of the intuition, the mysterious covenant between the soul and the soul of nature, that arduous craving to escape our earthly anchors that make possible our rising up to the sublime, to God.

Debussy's "Prelude of the afternoon of a Faun" was not only the preamble to a famous poem by Maeterlick, but even more so, in an almost prophetic anticipation, the "Prelude to the 20th century."

♪ Featured Music

Claude Debussy (1862-1918), *L'après midi d'un Faune* **(1894)**
Debussy was and is French—in fact, he signed his work and letters with "Musicien Français," French musician, as to not leave doubt in anyone's mind. His cradle stood in St-Germain en Laye, a suburb of Paris. Early on, at the Music Conservatoire, he was known as an eccentric dandy who liked to annoy his teachers with far-out chord combinations. Meanwhile he frequented the symbolists, poets and artists, and refined his own artistic taste, while frugally trying to live the life of an epicurist with hedonistic tendencies.

As of 1905 he became more reclusive, partly because of difficulties in his private life, but also being keenly aware that new musical expressions were being formulated (Schoenberg and Stravinsky) and soon he was groping to find new ways for his own work. He sensed that being or staying an "impressionist" was like being in a cul-de-sac, a turn-around without exit.

This "Prelude à l'après-midi d'un faune" was Debussy's first and most enduring work as an Impressionist. It created such a sensation, that it was repeated immediately at its premiere, an unusual occurrence. Everything was stunningly non-traditional with unconventional approaches to melody, harmony, rhythm and timbre. It was as if they heard a flute for the first time! It starts with a flute, all by itself, very delicate, supported only for the last note with a subtle chord. Immediately a rest follows, keeping the music in suspense, while savoring the moment. It's not what was said, but how it was said that became most important.

This work was in so many ways anti-German, which was welcomed in Paris, especially after the humiliating defeat in the 1870 Franco-Prussian war. The French felt proud again. Everything was novel; the orchestration lost its bombastic German heaviness; the melody was amazingly new, at times capricious, or just drawn in simple lines over exquisite harmonies; the harmony, Debussy's most characteristic feature, is in direct opposition to the former chromatic overwrought German ponderousness; the rhythm too lost its tyrannical German downbeat, and now either resorts to free flowing rhythms, or syncopations, that erases the old formality of artfully crafted polyrhythmic devises; Debussy's forms are no longer subject to developments or worn scholastic sonata-forms, but is friendlier to the dance-forms or the multifaceted basic design of the ABA.

Although it only takes about nine minutes to perform, rarely has so much been said in so short a time.

Claude Debussy: Prelude to the Afternoon of a Faun (1894)

A B A' form

A.   0:00 Solo flute - main melody
          Followed by harp glissando and soft horn calls. Pause. Harp and horns repeated.
          Flute and oboe play different variations of the main melody, given over to the clarinet.
          3: 41 New oboe melody that lead to a climax of short duration.
B   4:56 Broad legato melody in long notes, leads eventually to a renewed climax.
A.   6:46 Main melody in augmentation—solos of oboe, staccato woodwinds, harp and oboe, English horn and harp glissando.
          8:03 hand bells. Flutes in main melody and solo violin and oboe eventually bring the main melody to a close.
          9:46 main melody sounded far off in the violins, ending the piece with most delicate colors fading into silence.

Maurice Ravel (1875-1937), *Alborado del Gracioso* (1905)
Ravel saw the light in the Basque part of the French Pyrenees. Although in many ways he was Debussy's counterpart, he never was in close contact with him.

Ravel quickly found his personal style. In later years, his music had a daring, abstract feel. In fact he is less "romantic" than his predecessor Debussy. His harmonies have sharper dissonances, his melodies, though clear and simple, follow the modal scales without the despotic tendencies of a leading tone. His rhythms have distinct traces of dances, especially the waltz, the Spanish habanera or even jazz, as in the last movement of his concerto for piano. Ravel's music is quintessentially French: charming, entertaining, but never shallow, with a generous portion of the fantastic and visionary.

This piece "Alborado del Gracioso" brings us directly into a Spanish marketplace, where a guitar, singer and dancer provide the music for the "morning song of the jester." No, not a story is told, but as Oscar Wilde said "it is the spectator, not life, that art really mirrors." The piece, originally for piano, is written in ABA form. The outer panels have a strong rhythmic drive, the middle section quiet like a summer morning. Ravel was not as prolific as other composers, but much is memorable; his Bolero, Pavane for the Dead Infante, and not to overlook his very demanding Piano Concerto for the Left Hand. We cannot forget his marvelous orchestration of Mussorgsky's Pictures at an Exhibition.

Ottorino Respighi (1879-1936), *Fountains of Rome* **(1926)]**
This is Respighi's best and most well-known work. He juggled the colors of the orchestra as well as Rimsky-Korsakov, his teacher. The latter instructed him when Respighi was living in St. Petersburg, Russia. When he returned to his native Italy and lived in Rome he wrote three extensive Suites on the Pines of Rome, Fountains of Rome and Festivals of Rome. All the fountains are sketched at that time of day when their character is most alluring. "The Giulia Valley Fountain" is highlighted at daybreak, as peaceful pastorale aubade. "The Fountain of the Tritone" summons the troops of naiads and tritons in the early morning to a dance in a piazza full of sun and life. "The Trevi Fountain at Midday" is the one we all know from motion pictures with Sophia Loren. In our imagination we see Neptune's chariot drawn by sea-horses passing by in a solemn procession. And finally "The Medici Fountain at Sunset" is readying for the night with some tolling bells and rustling leaves. A spectacular view under the long shadows of the evening sun.

Paul Dukas (1865-1936), *The Sorcerer's Apprentice* **(1897)**
Paul Dukas lived all his life in Paris. This "Sorcerer" is unquestionably his best work. This symphonic scherzo gives a musical vision of Goethe's mordant ballad of the same name. The old sorcerer gives his pupil the responsibility to look after the workplace, while he was doing some errands. No sooner is he gone than the young magician wants to take a bath and being lazy, decides to let the

broom do the work. He knows the starting formula so the magic broom brings on the pails of water, but it cannot stop when the bath is full, because the young man never learned the magic words to stop the action. So the pails keep coming and soon the place floods, and in his anger and despair he hacks the broom in half, hoping to stop its destructive action. Now there are two tireless workers! It is not difficult to imagine that everything will not cease until the old man comes home to exorcise the undesired spirits. Dukas' illustration of Goethe's ballad is rather comical, without really going into the depth of the message—the danger of calling unknown forces, which we cannot sufficiently control.

A mysterious beginning creates an atmosphere of suspense, until a clarinet and starts again only to keep on going with greater momentum—the spirits have heard their magic call and respond with action. The music is flowing as fast as the water in Goethe's ballad. After a while we hear some heavy, biting chords, the apprentice getting angry and frustrated. After splitting the broom in half and a momentary hesitation in the music, the theme goes on with renewed force, and through a canon, indicates the two brooms working overtime. When the master sorcerer appears and speaks the needed hocus pocus, the music falls still, with regret at first, the bassoons struggle and the clarinets try to continue the fun, but it's over. Two quick measures and the piece has ended. Walt Disney in his "Fantasia" made the most of it in a unique visualization.

Gustav Holst (1874-1934), *The Planets* **(1916)**
Holst is an English composer of partly Swedish descent. His mother was an English pianist. He studied besides music, Hindu scriptures and astrology. His interests in the latter germinated the idea of "The Planets." The work underwent a long gestation period. Because of the war's restrictions it received a private performance under Adrian Boult in 1918. Although its early history is one of fragmentary performances, the work was destined to become his most popular work. Even though conceived before the war, the powerful depiction of "Mars, the Bringer of War," was an awesome foreboding of the approaching cataclysm. It is quickly followed by "Venus, the Bringer of Peace," still slightly Wagnerian. As of "Mercury, the Winged Messenger," we enter into the silvery sound-world of the Impressionists. As the great impressionist historian John Rewald puts it, "dots and commas capture the glistening atmosphere." The result is a deliberate sketchiness that is beguiling to the modem ear. "Jupiter, the Bringer of Old Age" a procession walks relentlessly to its rather surprising goal. "Uranus, the Magician" very much lives in the enchantment of witchcraft and finally "Neptune, the Mystic" plunges us into the world of Nirvana, of beatific vision, of infinite ecstasy. The addition of exquisite orchestration, Holst adds a women's choir,

singing only vowels, embellishing its airy-light elegance. England had joined the modern world.

Aaron Copland (1900-1990), *Appalachian Spring* **(1943-49)**
Copland, born in Brooklyn, is perhaps the first American composer to achieve international fame. He traveled as a young man, with barely enough money, to Paris to study with Madame Boulanger, a prominent teacher. While in Paris, Gershwin was there, writing his "American In Paris," made famous by Gene Kelly, the dancer. Madame Boulanger encouraged Copland to use American idioms, cowboys songs, folktunes, revival hymns, white and Negro spirituals and of course jazz. While in Paris he not only established familiarity with Debussy and Stravinsky, but also with American Jazz, which was and still is popular in the City of Lights. Later in life Copland's music was more acerbic and abstract in tone and thereby lost the affection of the general public. He became increasingly bitter. Nevertheless his music is American par excellence.

In 1943 Copland was commissioned to compose music for a ballet for Martha Graham's modem dance company. He selected a scene set around the celebration of spring in the hills of Pennsylvania. Rather than telling a story, Copland evokes some moods and feelings by a young farmer's couple, at the beginning of their life together. Copland always had a diverse audience in mind stating that "…it made no sense to ignore them and to continue writing as if they did not exist. I felt that it was worth the effort to see if I couldn't say what I had to say in the simplest possible terms." To that ideal Copland lived up superbly and because of that commitment, this work became his most appreciated score. Especially noteworthy are the variations on a Shaker hymn "Simple Gifts," first stated as is, then with more motion, then as a call, followed by horses trotting and finally as a congregational hymn sung in church, with full organ and assertive big pedal-basses. A real tour de force. Copland had it made.

William Grant Still (1895-1978), *Afro-American Symphony* **(1933)**
Still was an Afro-American musician born in Woodville, Mississippi who died in Los Angeles. As Earl Calloway relates with regret at his death "a great musician sleeps and this generation never knew him."

His work consists of more than a hundred orchestral pieces, five symphonies, several operas and many works for chorus, most of it published and performed. He wrote much for films and television (music for "Gunsmoke" and the "Perry Mason Show") and also the well-known tune "Stormy Weather." Most of the credit for being who he was he gives to Varese, the teacher who most influenced him.

In 1933 Still writes "It wasn't until I went to Memphis that I discovered the real quality of African-American music." Until then American blacks thought that the blues were immoral, but Still thought otherwise and used them most eloquently in his Afro-American Symphony.

Still adhered to "established forms, as practiced by the classicists" as he said. The first movement is in a straightforward sonata-allegro form—complete with two contrasting themes, development and recapitulation. From the very outset of the first theme there is a pronounced blues character. Most interesting is that in the recapitulation the second theme, which appears now first, is transformed into a real jazzy swing version, featuring the trumpet section. The coda ends the first movement in a subdued fashion.

Although Still employed black American idioms, including spirituals, blues, worksongs, ragtime and jazz rhythms, the tenor of the work has a definite "impressionistic" feel. Besides being an interesting piece it is noteworthy to mention that it was the first symphonic work by a black American to be performed by a major symphony orchestra, the Rochester Philharmonic (1931).

Still adds as a kind of post-script: "He who develops his God-given gifts with a view to aiding humanity, manifests truth." A worthy goal for a great composer!

Characteristics of Impressionistic Art and Music

F = Fluid and fleeting; the main focus are mist, haze, water, and ocean
R = Restrained sound and colors; sensuous, delicate, picturesque
A = Atmospheric: sets mood, feeling. Impression rather than storytelling
N = Nature is first and foremost teacher and inspiration
C = Colorful orchestration, often muted, hazy and pastel-like
E = Exquisite, exotic, and always beautiful as its main objective

20ᵗʰ Century

Dead he is not, but departed—
For the artist never dies.
Epitaph on the tombstone of
Albrecht Durer, Painter

Music and Art to 1960

The first half of the 20th century brought merciless change. Certainly the words—change, revolution and reactionary—all have been used throughout history, be it in the political arena or the art world. But changes during the 20th century seemed more profound, more disturbing, perhaps even more obnoxious. It is true that the change between Renaissance and Baroque was quite abrupt—Palestrina versus Monteverdi was quite a radical change. The chasm between the Baroque and Classical periods was equally deep and disturbing to their contemporaries—Bach and Haydn don't read from the same book. The breach separating Beethoven and Berlioz is even apparent to the non-musician. The dissimilarities between Brahms, Debussy, Stravinsky and Schoenberg are so great that it is difficult to accept that only a few years separate their works. A similar comparison could easily be established in the other arts with similar shocking results—that all changed the course of history.

In the first ten years of the 20th century we can hear the eruptions which engulf the world culture. Politically, wars were gathering steam, and the romantic "fin de siècle" feel was no longer to be soothed with illusions or by ignoring its deadening oppression. At first, nihilism and anarchy created despair, but eventually the strong were looking for different solutions. Communism, Nazism, Fascism all send their artists away, as the artist was always an irritant to society, especially to the dictator who discourages dissent.

The art that emerges will eventually be called Expressionism, a catchword evoking its opposition and change to the prevailing Impressionism and Romanticism. The contrast between trends is indeed far-reaching.

The Impressionist is influenced by the outer world, the immediate, the impression of the moment. The Expressionist begins with an idea; one that is so powerful that it is forced upon everyone, whether they are aware or not. All sentimentality, all illusion and dreams are negated and excluded. The pursuit of

Beauty, as the Impressionists and the Late-Romantic cultivated it, is now dead. It is an art of ideas. Reality is very often distorted; it is interpretation, rather than representation that counts. Very often elementary, even primitive means are used. The romanticization or illusionary dreams of the past ages are abandoned. Sometimes the ideas get so intense that basically anything goes to express them.

In the visual arts we have dozens of isms: Primitivism, Expressionism, Fauvism has artists like Gauguin, van Gogh, Munch, Matisse; Cubism with Picasso, Braque, Abstraction as practiced by Kandinsky, Mondrian; Surrealism performed by Duchamp, Arp, Dali. All these varied styles are more than just organized colors, these works express in diverse ways the tensions, frustrations and desperation of their time. The paintings of Picasso, the dances of Martha Graham, the sculptures of Rodin, the music of Stravinsky, the poems of e. e. cummings, all are stimuli of tension, trying to understand our personal involvement in the experience of life. It is a different involvement than spectators at a ballgame, who, when they lose, will fight it out in the bleachers with the partisans of the opposing team. In the arts, the involvement is more personal and more on the level of identification or connecting and understanding the meaning of the work before them. The works of art are capable of producing tension and the resolutions of these tension is attended by pleasure. These tensions can be elicited by strong stimuli e.g. by a fortissimo by a 120-piece orchestra, by deliberate distortions of familiar objects in the visual arts, or even clashing colors. We have the unique situation of relieving tension through tension.

In music melody, rhythm, harmony all undergo a metamorphic change that is no longer in tune with the standards of previous years. Nothing escapes the sweeping broom. Form, orchestration and the performance itself are no longer walking the same path of a few years past.

There is a similar trend in the other arts. Painting is dominated by such artists as the constantly changing Picasso, the cubism is the domain of Braque, abstractions are Kandinsky's, and the surrealism reigns with Dali and Mirò.

Music is equally led by opposing trends as well. Stravinsky and Schoenberg hardly have anything in common, Hindemith and Bartok set their own mark, and Milhaud and Prokofiev are never in the same ballpark. Let's not forget that jazz, with its pervasive influence on popular music, was gradually making inroads into the art music, already starting with Debussy and Ravel.

Stravinsky, while he is a cosmopolitan, is also very Russian. Russian music is wild, primitive, and visceral, infused with folksongs, inspired by fairy tales and most frequently dance (ballet) oriented. Stravinsky's first works have all the above trends, although the bite is especially ferocious in his "Rite of Spring." The latter work became the icon of the avant-garde. It was all there; the radicalization of rhythm, the merciless lashing with harsh chords and the last demolition of melody and form. After World War I, Stravinsky's palette became somewhat milder, even had a pasticcio-classic imitation in it. He called this his "return to Bach," although it never became music for everybody. Stravinsky was unquestionably an innovative leader and many of his epigones tried to navigate the same river.

Schoenberg is even more radical. He himself did not consider his innovations as revolutionary, but rather the inevitable next step in the evolution of German/Austrian music. But he accelerated that evolution. Schoenberg was an influential teacher with his Dodecaphonic system, popularly known as Twelve-Tone system. His most consequential students were Webern and Berg, both enthusiastic disciples of Schoenberg. This system will of course revolutionize the harmony, and the melody. The latter especially loses all its vocality under the weight of dizzying leaps and decimated rhythms. The aggressiveness of the chords has taken away any feeling, romantic or otherwise. That total cerebral abstraction is forbidding for most average listeners. Whatever we probe, the heart want to participate, and that music was considered heartless, cruel, brutal and cold. Nevertheless Schoenberg created a new language and never compromised even though he became more and more isolated.

His 12-tone system, though still in use, has lost some of its initial luster as it tends to be too intellectual and abstract. Since 1970 composers seldom use this system, and then only in short passages.

Paul Hindemith's contribution to the 20th century was equally decisive. At first his music was a complete negation of emotion and motoric in nature but as of 1934 his style became less eclectic and cerebral and adhered more to the human quality thereby enlarging his palette. His melody is unsentimental and has a distinct Baroque element: the perpetual motion with broad gestures. Although unromantic, his melodies never became stale or dry. As a true German, Hindemith is a contrapuntalist, weaving the inner voices into a logical whole. In that same vein Hindemith has a preponderance for the Baroque forms: fugue, passacaglia, variation and concerto. They all become his endearing treasure. Hindemith is a solid craftsman, decisively avoiding cheap sentimentality and exaggerated passion.

Bartók, on the other hand, is completely steeped in folk music. It is the substance and soul of his music. He never quotes the folk songs literally, but carefully siphons off their essence, especially their rhythms, infused as they are with characteristic patterns and unexpected accents and meters. Also the melodies have a uniqueness that Bartók uses to give his compositions a singular aspect. His harmony is razor sharp and has an explosive force as only Bartók can unleash. The forms Bartók works with are traditional, but their content is completely unorthodox in the broadest sense of the word.

Another contrasting two-some are Milhaud and Prokofiev.

Milhaud is by far the most gifted, prolific and spontaneous of the French group "Les Six." During and after World War I a group of young French composers interacted with Satie and the literary figure Cocteau to form the ideals of friendship and to counteract the pastels of the prevailing music, by trying to return to melodies with a sharper contour, to the precision of counterpoint, and with simplified expression. The Russian "Mighty Five" very much stayed together. In contrast "Les Six" went eventually all their own way, and three of them, Milhaud, Honegger and Poulenc, became the stalwarts of the PostImpressionistic French music. In contrast to Debussy's hesitant melodic lines, Milhaud's melodies are more sharply outlined, and at times a bit nonchalant and naughty. His harmony likes the rubbings of bitonality, not exactly new, but more consistent than the masters of the Late-Romantic period. His rhythms, influenced by South American dance music, jazz and other large rhythmic choruses, have an intoxicating effect upon his listeners. His kaleidoscopic talent, strengthened by technical mastery had an enormous following, especially among the youngest generation of American composers.

Comparison of Prokofiev to any other modem composer may not always fall in his favor, as Prokofiev kept some strong ties to the classical traditions, more so than Stravinsky, Hindemith, Schoenberg, Milhaud or even Bartók. His most beautiful pages are devoted to the piano, some ballet music and some memorable moments in his comic opera "The Love for Three Oranges" with the famous march and scherzo. His spontaneity and pointed humor are most typical in his Classical Symphony, the best serum in a world suffering from too much Skriabinism. As so many Russian composers, Prokofiev addresses also the younger crowd and writes a most delightful "Peter and the Wolf" without compromising his technique or style.

It is difficult to measure the impact jazz had upon the art music. Jazz is American bred, New Orleans the cradle, but soon had a world market appeal. The jazz rhythms imperceptibly at first, began to seep into the art music. Debussy used it as a novelty, Ravel became more daring and eventually many composers were mesmerized by this fascinating rhythmic attraction. Although Europe had been the center of "new music," four of its greatest exponents, Stravinsky, Schoenberg, Hindemith, and Bartók fled the horrors of Hitler's Nazism. All of them, except perhaps Bartók, introduced jazz rhythms and jazz idioms into their music. They often found inspiration in jazz and although the influence was intermittent it is too frequent to be overlooked.

♪ *Featured Music*

Igor Stravinsky (1882-1971), *Rite of Spring Part I* **(1913)**
The "Rites" impact upon music cannot be overestimated. Even Stravinsky himself was astonished. All sentimentality and charm is literally mercilessly obliterated, leaving feelings of exhaustion and frustration. Melody becomes secondary—except perhaps at the beginning where a lonesome Lithuanian tune is partially quoted. Later, some short fragments of Russian folktunes are interjected, even repeated a couple of times without further reference.

But it is the rhythm that dominates the piece. Relentless, primitive, yes the soul of all Stravinsky's music, this visceral force is the motor of most of his work. It drums like magical incantations with violent outbursts of energy, forcing itself on the listener. Nothing is left to convention. The first beats are no longer accented, as syncopations, unconventional accents, irregular measures push implacably against the parameters of former years. Stravinsky's rhythm is rooted in the dance: no wonder that most of his music was written for ballet. Only when he starts dipping into the forms of the Renaissance or Baroque will his rhythm be tamed, although many times we hear the old rhythmic cadences so typical of his music.

Stravinsky talking of the "Rite of Spring" relates that the idea came as a "fleeting vision" while he was completing "The Firebird" in 1910.

The Introduction is the reawakening of nature. It starts with the bassoon at the top of its register, croaking out a Lithuanian folk tune. No clearly defined pulse gives the impression of chaos, reiterated by sharp dissonances. The end of the Introduction comes to a piercing climax, abruptly broken by the solo bassoon repeating its initial tune.

Then comes the dance of youths and young girls, the omens of Spring; a very rhythmic, rapid pounding dissonant chords with irregular accents jabbed by eight horns giving a feel of primordial confusion and disorder. Some snatches of a Russian folk tune appear, the variation is less in the changing melodies than in changing colors and rhythmic patterns.

The pace of the Ritual of Abduction becomes more and more frenzied and furious. Violent blows on the timpani and bass drum sweep the music to a ferocious pitch. Unbridled tension is generated by powerful accents and irregular beats bringing this section to an overwhelming climax.

The whole Rite of Spring glorifies the power of rhythm in its most animalistic form. It arouses excitement, rage, mania and tension to a very high degree, making it a most unpleasant and even painful experience.

The Rite of Spring was written for an enormous orchestra enlarged with a great array of percussion instruments. Its premiere was a disaster. People were so aroused that fist fights broke out and threw many objects at the orchestra so that they had to stop playing. Stravinsky himself walked the streets in Paris in utter desolation. Stravinsky never wrote a work like it, and no composer dared tread that primitivistic path again.

Igor Stravinsky, *Symphony of Psalms* (1930)
Why Stravinsky gradually changed course in the early 1920s is somewhat of a mystery. Strangely he did not return to the Romantic's fairyland, instead he invoked the music of the Baroque and Renaissance. He called it his "return to Bach." Known as Neoclassicism, it is an obvious misnomer, perhaps Neo-Baroque would have been more appropriate, although Neoclassicism is more an attitude than a style.

In this composition brass predominates and sweeter sounding violins, violas and clarinets are totally eliminated from his palette. By this time Stravinsky had renounced the brutal dissonants, although the work is still decidedly anti-romantic. The second movement is a fugue, in which he is transcending the contrapuntal language. The last movement obviously the most approachable for the general audience—in fact he wrote the work for the Boston Philharmonic's anniversary, and the request was to write something popular or at least accessible! It is a beautiful work. He succeeded with the charge.

Towards the end of his career Stravinsky made yet another change in style and started composing in the 12-tone system, most amazing since he had fought this system as being sterile and cerebral.

Arnold Schoenberg (1874-1954), *Vorgefühle* from *Five pieces for Orchestra* (1909)
Schoenberg is an Austrian-born composer who lived in Germany until forced out by the Nazis as a Jew and a composer of decadent music. In 1933 he came to the U.S. He died in Los Angeles. He composed first in the Wagnerian style "Trans-

figured Night." As of 1908 he developed a "system" that radicalized the music profoundly. (Within the octave are twelve notes, using the black and white keys. None should be repeated until all the others are heard first.) Schoenberg felt it was necessary to simplify the musical language of the melodically and harmonically overloaded works of the later German Romanticism. He eliminated the distinction between consonance and dissonance and thereby the need to resolve the chords to pre-existing rules of harmony. By this new system the melodies were freer and could be interwoven without worrying about their clashing. The greatest stumbling block is just that, his harmonies are a constant heaping of dissonant chords.

The Five Pieces for Orchestra were the first ones written in 12-tone system for full orchestra. And revolutionary pieces they were. Although the 'title' of the work was suggested to him by his publisher, it expresses in some odd way the feel of anticipation. Is this the music of the future or a foreboding of WWI?

This piece is short as are most 12-tone pieces. The introduction is ½ minute and the rest only three times as long. The introduction seems very bewildering with an inordinate amount of musical ideas which then merge into a steady ostinato bass (three notes repeated incessantly). The sound becomes increasingly louder and intense, crashing into a snarling chord of trombones and tuba. All in all an interesting piece.

Schoenberg, Pierrot lunaire, *Poetry by Albert Giraud (Belgium)* (1912)
This is the capstone of Schoenberg's atonal system. Scored for soprano, it has an unusual performance style, called Sprechstimme, halfway between singing and speaking. The accompaniment has four instruments with piano. The poetry, with its frequently bizarre and unearthly imagery and its deep, often emotional content is required reading to understand the intent of Schoenberg's music. Was it meant as a poetry reading in some sophisticated cabaret?

A painter, Schoenberg also details grisly deformed figures on his post-war canvases. This he repeats in his later extremely emotional and horror-filled works like the cantata A Survivor from Warsaw (1947). The latter composition includes Hebrew, the languages of his religion, to which he had returned; German, his native tongue; English, his adopted language in the United States. The 6-minute cantata is heartrending, especially when the male chorus chants the prayer "Shema Yisroel" sung for the Jewish martyrs in their last agonizing hours. This is music way beyond the strains of the entertainment music of department stores.

Paul Hindemith (1895-1963), *Mathis der Mahler* (1934)

Hindemith was bom in Frankfurt, Germany. As soon as the Nazis came to power he was banned as musically "degenerate," a repudiation that was totally absurd. Once he formulated his theoretical position, Hindemith's music from the middle of the 1930s until his death remained remarkably consistent in style; he adhered to it most faithfully. After the chaotic transition period from about 1905 to 1925, when the music somehow restabilized into a balanced, mature and comprehensive style, is when Hindemith wrote some of his best work. His production was torrential, and his intelligent curiosity led him to examine all genres. His music is definitely un-romantic, although he gives preference to a milder dissonance, more so than Stravinsky, Schoenberg or Bartok.

Mathis Grünewald, (c. 1475-1528) the controversial painter who was caught in the conflicts of the Reformation, had to choose between painting or taking part in the Peasant's Rebellion. His masterpiece is the altarpiece for a church in Isenheim. The terrible contorted figure of the Crucified Christ is very intense in its passionate expression of the Visions of St. Bridget. Although neglected for four centuries, his paintings are now appreciated for their Late Gothic imagery. Only a few paintings of his are known.

By writing about a German historical figure, the painter Mathis Grünewald, Hindemith tried to restore his reputation. He had been under severe scrutiny by the Nazi regime, but Hindemith's ploy did not work and the premiere was forbidden in Berlin, although the famous conductor Furtwangler played it is 1934 under horrendous tumult and was himself severely reprimanded. By then, Hindemith was removed from his teaching post and told to leave the country.

Each of the movements represents one of the three panels of Grunewald's masterpiece, the Isenheim altar triptych; the Angelic concert, The Entombment, and The Temptations of Saint Anthony.

In the Angelic Concert Hindemith used an old folksong "Three Angels were Singing" which begins in solemn tone and later returns at the climax of contrapuntal developments of three themes—one for each angel.

The Entombment is a touchingly moving peaceful piece, the Pieta of the three panels.

The last movement, The Temptations of Saint Anthony, is the most involved piece. After a fierce and vehement opening, the piece moves on with a quick, thrusting drive in which eventually the chant of "Lauda Sion" is introduced, superimposed upon the rapidly moving strings. Eventually the symphony ends with a rousing glorious "Alleluia."

Mathis, the painter, and Hindemith, the musician, both reached a triumphant end after their resistance to unyielding authorities. A great piece within the enormous production by one of the pillars of the 20th century.

Béla Bartók (1881-1945), *Music for Strings, Percussion and Celesta* **(1936)**
Bartók is through and through Hungarian, even though he settled in the U.S.A., in 1940, dying in New York City a poor man. Partly in association with Kodaly, he collected and edited Hungarian folk songs, which style he used in his compositions. It is difficult to categorize or to try to tie him into a "school" as Bartók's music is extremely personal and unique. One of his best works just before his decision to move to the United States is undoubtedly his Music for Strings. Although Bartok was always partial to the piano, his second love lies with the strings. After all his last works were for strings!

The Music for Strings is one of his most powerful and moving works, conceived for a double string orchestra, piano, harp, drums, cymbals, timpani, and celesta. An imaginative sonority ensues and even the most commonly used forms also undergo a mutation that brings them new life.

The first movement is a fugue which runs the complete circle of keys until the entrance of the celeste and now the fugue theme is the inversion of itself.

In contrast to the mystical sounding fugue the second movement, in sonata form, has enormous rhythmic power and the themes pass antiphonically from one group to another gloriously playful.

The third movement is a characteristically "night music" as only Bartók can write. The xylophone solo opens with a most unusual and poetically effective accelerando, merging into a timpani roll and glissando leading to a plaintive viola figure, expanded upon by the other strings. The strings give way to a piano, harp and celeste trio, only to be intercepted by a return of the strings and a cymbal crash.

The final movement is essentially a dance in an assertive Bulgarian rhythm. The pace is high and the rhythmic force strong and direct. After a short reprieve when the sound almost disappears, the Bulgarian dance resumes with renewed and augmented energy and vigor ending the piece in a burst of forceful activity.

Because Bartók was always sure of what he wanted, the work was completed in just ten weeks, even though it is a complex and substantial score. The next year he wrote Sonata for Two Pianos and Percussion, and performed it with his wife, Ditta Pasztory, on January 16, 1938.

This work turned out to be one of the very last Bartók composed before leaving for the United States. He vowed that he would not compose again, so disillusioned was he. He relented only when he accepted a commission from Boston's conductor, Serge Koussevitzky, writing his Concerto for Orchestra. This was in May 1943. Less than a year later Bartok died, without seeing his beloved Hungary again and leaving some works to be completed by his associate Tibor Serly. Bartok's contribution to the 20th century is difficult to evaluate, but certainly in his Concerto for Orchestra and in the Music for Strings, Percussion and Celesta he reaches a new perfection in the fullness and nobility of its melody, rhythm, harmony and form. These great masterworks are among the outstanding compositions of the twentieth century.

Sergei Prokofiev (1891-1953), *Peter and the Wolf* (1936)

This Russian composer and pianist was a pupil of Rimsky-Korsakov. From 1918 he lived mostly abroad until 1934, when he settled again in the Soviet Union. There, in 1936, he was severely reprimanded along with Shostakovich, Khachaturian, Miaskovsky, and others. His work was considered too "formalistic," which Premier Stalin found offensive. Interestingly he wrote a letter acknowledging his lack of melody, tonality and other "shortcomings." Even his lovely work "Peter and the Wolf" was considered by the Soviets as "garbage." Nevertheless Prokofiev conformed and all the official restrictions did not prove damaging to his output.

This piece, usually performed with narration, is a delightful composition with children in mind. Peter, the wolf, the grandfather, the cat, the bird and the hunters all get their own melody and only a witty Prokofiev attains great beauty while being faithful to his own gift. His art always abounds with enthusiasm that he infuses with genuine warmth.

In 1945 Prokofiev suffered a serious accident and never fully recovered, although he kept on working in spite of doctor's orders and he accomplished an amazing amount even in his last years. As a final irony, Prokofiev died the same day as his tormentor Stalin!

Darius Milhaud (1892-1974), *Le boeuf sur le toit* **(1919)**
Milhaud is a true Frenchman, born in Aix-en-Provence, the South of France, far from the City of Lights, Paris. His output is simply prodigious and his activities no less diverse as a teacher, conductor, and above all a great raconteur. During the First World War he served at the French Embassy in Rio De Janeiro as Paul Claudel's assistant. But no sooner was he in Brazil he wrote several pieces with Latin-American rhythms, many becoming ever-popular successes while proving his extraordinary versatility and creativity. He would remember those Latin rhythms as many of his later compositions have a Latin-American influence.

His "Christopher Columbus" (1928) is now considered his greatest composition, one of the many works in collaboration with his friend, the poet Paul Claudel. Milhaud expresses himself more fully in his dramatic works. Milhaud's work is expressionistic, but very different and less pessimistic then a Schoenberg or any other central European composer. His work is beautiful, not because he is intelligent, but because his intelligence communicates emotion to us. His art never is offensive as he never put himself on the path of egocentricity or eccentricity. He remains spontaneous and his language stays tonal and relatively free of chromatic notes. Even his rhythm is not restricted to Latin-American, but also African-American, Indian and Jazz are very much on the menu.

To compare Milhaud with any other contemporary composer is useless as it is difficult to classify the composer of Le Boeuf sur le Toit. The latter piece is from 1919 with Jean Cocteau as the producer and décor by no less a painter than Raoul Dufy. The title "The Bull on the roof" has no special meaning, nor does the music have any dramatic action, except that it is a clever piece in the rondo form with piquant touches of polytonality and driven by popular Brazilian rhythms. As Milhaud himself said in his autobiography, Notes sans Musique "it is a merry, unpretentious divertissement by a strolling musician."

Olivier Messiaen (1908-1991), *Turangalila-Symphonie* **(1945)**
Messiaen was born in Avignon. His mother was the poet Cecile Sauvage and his father a professor of literature. He called himself "a Frenchman of the mountains, like Berlioz." In 1931 he was appointed organist at the Trinite church Paris, a post he held for fifty-five years. Being an organist, his first great masterpiece "La Nativite" was for organ. In 1936 he was co-founder of Jeune-France, a group of four composers which represented the avant-garde at the time. In 1940 he was a German prisoner of war and during his captivity he wrote "Quatuor pour la fin du temps," a quartet "for the end of time," and he premiered it for and with his compatriots in a prison camp!

By the end of the war Messiaen had a great influence upon the younger European composers and many studied under him, among them Boulez and Stockhausen.

The three main sources of his techniques of composition are 1) rhythm, greatly based upon Hindu rhythmic formulas and also by artificially increasing or decreasing the note lengths; 2) artificial scales, Indian scales and Gregorian chant scales, yielding new harmonies; and 3) his inordinate use of actual bird songs, some notations taken down of birds he heard during his extensive travels. He is a real pioneer of total organization, of total control. And even though melody, rhythm and harmonies all are "serialized," the actual sound seems random and at times chaotic. Besides those technical innovations, his music is deeply mystical, which contributes to the emotional detachment. Some of his music contains long melodies of inhuman slowness, reaching into the obscure regions of the subconscious.

His orchestration is an imitation of the Balinese gamelan—by the way, Messiaen is the only composer who emphasized the need to study Asiatic and African music. Messiaen's orchestra always demands the extreme, especially in the rhythm section.

In his Turangalila, or love song, Messiaen not only introduces all aforementioned technical innovations but also the principle of three rhythmic personages:

The first theme has an oppressive, terrifying brutality of ancient Mexican art, the "statue theme."

The second theme is gentle with caressing clarinets, depicting a delicate orchid, the "flower theme."

The third theme is the most important one, the "love theme," sometimes fast and passionate, sometimes tirelessly slow and endless.

The introduction gives the essence of the complete cycle. The first two themes are heard: "the statue theme" on the trombones, and the "flower theme" on the clarinets very oft. After a lengthy piano solo cadenza comes the main part of the movement. This section ends with an immutable "statue theme" that brings it to a stern conclusion.

Characteristics of 20th Century Art and Music (1910-1960)

<u>M</u> = merciless, obnoxious
<u>O</u> = outburst of emotion
<u>D</u> = dissonant, harsh, cerebral, abstract
<u>E</u> = experimental, expressionism
<u>R</u> = revolutionary, reactionary
<u>N</u> = non-existent tonality, radicalized rhythm, un-singable melody
<u>I</u> = inflexible, not after beauty, but ideas
<u>S</u> = shocking primitivism and many other unusual means are used
<u>M</u> = multimedia, mixed media and minimalism all are new concepts

Timeline for 20th Century

1901	Transatlantic cable
1903	Wright brothers fly their airplane at Kitty Hawk
1912	Titanic sinks
1914-18	World War 1
1915	Hollywood movies
1917	Russian Revolution
1920	flappers—the "roaring twenties"
1922	King Tut's tomb discovered in Egypt
1922	Fascism in Italy
1927	Lindberg flies to Paris
1929	Depression, stock market crash
1931	"talkies," movies with sound capabilities
1933	Hitler in power
1935	Hammond organ invented
1936	Civil War in Spain—Picasso paints Guernica
1937	+ Gershwin (was 39) + Ravel (was 62)
1939	Mass emigration of European artists, scientists and musicians to U.S.
1940-45	World War II
1985-88	Van Gogh's "Irises" sold for $53.9 million. Renoir's "Au Moulin de la Galette" sold for $78. 1. Four works by Renoir and Van Gogh sold for $270 million.

Music and Art Since 1960

Every work of art is the child of its age...
Which can never be repeated.
—Wassily Kandinsky

Did the music and the other arts change after 1960? "The world has changed less since Jesus Christ, than it has in the last thirty years" said Charles Péguy in 1913. What would he think now?

Of course, by 1960 most of the great and influential composers had gone to their eternal reward—Debussy in 1918; Satie, Janácek, and Puccini in the twenties; Ravel, Berg, Holst, Respighi, and Gershwin in the thirties; Bartók, de Falla, and Webern in the forties; Ives, Prokofiev, Schoenberg, Weill, Vaughan Williams, Sibelius, Villa-Lobos in the fifties. The long parade of masterworks such as Pierrot Lunaire, Le Sacre du Printemps, Wozzeck, Bolero, the Planets, Rhapsody in Blue, the Concerto for Orchestra, La Vida Breve, was halted by the 1960s. Most of these works had been part of a deliberate break with the past. But that had happened before, when Tristan, Pelleás or Symphonie Fantastique or Beethoven's last quartets were first heard, those works had a profound effect.

Who was left?

Of the older generation there were Varèse, (1883-1965) who after his Poème èlectronique (1958) was seventy-five years old and near the end of his creative life. This had been a triumph after a very revolutionary career—it had been performed at the World's Fair in Brussels, with Le Corbusier (architect) and Xenakis as his assistant. Milhaud (1892-1974), Dallapiccola (1901-1975), Orff (1895-1982), Poulenc (1873-1963), Walton (1902-1982), Hindemith (1895-1963), Kodály (1882-1967) all were still with us, but most had fallen silent after their respective great careers.

Only one, Igor Stravinsky, (1882-1971) was ready and able for more. In fact, he had recently changed his style and was diligently writing music in the twelve-tone technique. In so many ways Stravinsky now wrote music with the most advanced compositional tendencies of the '50s and '60s. This was a remarkable achievement for an octogenarian. And yet, Stravinsky's stamp and flavor remained clearly audible. His portfolio of masterworks was enlarged with The Flood, Variations for Orchestra, A Sermon, a Narrative and a Prayer, Abraham and Isaac and Requiem Canticle, all composed using the twelve-tone system. It is significant that Stravinsky should begin writing serial and dodecaphonic music within one year of Schoenberg's death. This brought renewed prominence to a wilting musical language that was under severe criticism as being too cerebral and sterile.

At first, most of the early sixties music stayed close to the lean, "modern" sound of Anton Webern, rather than the heavy and thick texture of Schoenberg. Especially prominent are Boulez and Stockhausen, who both adhered to the new serialism. In the same camp was Messiaen, and in the United States, Milton Babbit. The complexity of their music is difficult to grasp for the average listener. In serialism, all the musical elements, melody, harmony, rhythm and the actual sound are all tightly organized and controlled.

On the other hand, we also saw the opposite. Chance music, anything goes! Anything, be it melody, rhythm and harmony and even tone color are in the game of chance; "aleatory" in professional parlance. The performer is in charge and can play certain passage in random order, with their own selected rhythmic pattern, while tossing coins in choosing short groups of pitches. John Cage became their guru. For example, a composition entitled 4'33" (1952) required not to make a single sound for four minutes and thirty three seconds, while the performer was turning pages as if looking at a printed score! Obviously, after a while, coughing, whispering, and shuffling fill the air. Music! In another instance, his Imaginary Landscape (1951) Cage wanted twelve radios, randomly playing any music, or even announcing news or weather. Karl Heinz Stockhausen's Piano Piece #11 (1956) has nineteen short segments that can be played in any order, so that no two performances will be the same.

Minimalist Music is yet another development in music, reacting against the complexities of the serialist and the absurdities of chance music. The main characteristics of this music are that the melodies are incessantly repeated, the rhythms very constant and just droning away, and the harmonies rather simplistic. Steve Reich, Philip Glass, and John Adams are the main proponents of this development. Most of their music has a trance-like, hypnotic effect and many young people who adhere to Indian religions or New Age philosophies identify strongly with this music.

Another shift in the compositorial procedures is the widespread quotation of traditional music from the past. References in music are not new at all; after all, Debussy liked to quote Wagner, Berg in Lulu quoted Wagner's Tristan and in his Violin concerto he brought in a Bach chorale. By far the most famous models are Pulcinella by Stravinsky, in which he fills in missing measures of a manuscript from Pergolesi with his own, and The Fairy's Kiss, also by Stravinsky, with numerous themes taken from Tchaikovsky. Charles Ives enjoys quotations and some of his Symphonies have a real collage effect. The difference is that now everyone seems to be doing it. Lucas Foss, Luciano Berio, and even Ellen Taaffe Zwilich all weave pre-Baroque, Baroque or other borrowed material into the fabric of their own music.

Without a doubt the influence of jazz and rock has been strong. That had happened already, in the early years of the 20th century. Debussy, Ravel, Hindemith, Milhaud and Stravinsky all were touched by popular music in some way. But that penetration of jazz became less evident after 1960, except that rock began to raise its head. Interesting that some rock musicians like Frank Zappa, Glenn Branca, Laurie Anderson, all started out in the pop-field, but now are working on less commercial projects. Also composers such as Leonard Bernstein, Stephen Sondheim, Andrew Lloyd Webber and Claude-Michel Schonberg of "Les Miserable," all use techniques associated with art music in combination with Latin-American, jazz and rock music elements.

The invention or better yet, the development of the synthesizer also had quite some impact upon the composer's scene. The creation of new instruments or the modification of old ones usually moved hand in hand with the expansion of the creative output. The violin, the piano, the valves of the brass instruments, the saxophone or improvements on the woodwind instruments, all sparked new possibilities and enlarged literature for these instruments. Until now the dominant figures such as Schoenberg and Stravinsky were still committed to the acoustical instruments. It was not until after World War II that such experimental instruments as "noise makers," or the Ondes Martinot or even the so called musique concrète (taped music with conventional instruments) became a thing of the past.

By 1960 what had taken hours to produce in a "classical studio" was now possible in "real" time on a synthesizer. There are nonetheless serious disadvantages; the synthesizer is still in its infancy, as many sounds have a prepackaged quality that produce a certain sameness, and in some ways is still tedious to operate. But ever since the Switched-On Bach on the Moog, the synthesizer has become a household word. Many composers went on to have mixed media, synthesizer and other "live" musicians, either in dialogue or along with. Composers like Cage, Stockhausen, Davidovsky and Babbitt are the most prominent in that field.

Although the computer shows some promise to actually "compose" music, that interest has waned somewhat. Perhaps it is too single-minded to be flexible enough for "free" composition.

And the future? It is possible that we will never see a unified style again as was the case during the Renaissance, the Baroque, the Classical and even the Romantic eras. It appears as if we will see the continuation of a multiplicity of different expressions. The knifing harshness of the early 20th century has been largely softened and mellowed long with the apparent rediscovery of tonality. Especially the so-called new Age style is using the tonalities in their most pure and serene form—no more biting dissonances, no more uncomfortable and cruel chords, no intrusion of chromatic or other "foreign" notes. Rather than the proverbial "epater le bourgeois," (impress the layman), there is now a sense of strongly profiled melodies, profuse orchestration and a genuine concern for direct personal expression. Are we entering a new Romantic Era?

The Other Arts since 1960

Similar trends as in music are observable in the visual arts.

The old stand-by isms are still operational. Fauvism with Matisse and Vlaminck; Cubism with Picasso and Braque; Surrealism with Miro, Dali, Magritte and Delvaux; Abstract Expressionism with Pollock, Kline, Rothko and de Kooning; Pop Art with Warhol, Post-Modernism with Philip Pearlstein, Frank Stella, Anselm Kiefer, Keith Haring. Minimalism became the newest development in the art world, as had been in music. Most prominent minimalists are: Richard Serra, Ronald Bladen, and also many women artists, such as Jackie Winsor, Anne Truitt and others.

Sculpture became more prominent, not only in the hands of Picasso, Miro, David Smith, but especially Claes Oldenburg who did what he called "non-feasible" sculptures, as the 74,000 pound Flashlight standing beam-end down on the University of Nevada campus, the 68-foot-high match Cover for the Summer Olympics in Barcelona, Spain, or the 45-foot-tall Clothespin in front of City Hall in Philadelphia.

And then there is the conceptual artist Christo—famous for wrapping Biscayne Bay islands in pink plastic and planting thousands of open umbrellas in California and Japan. In his latest project he puts the infamous Reichstag, the Berlin Parliament of the Nazis, literally under wraps: a million square feet of silver fabric, tied with ten miles of blue ribbon.

Architecture had just lost Frank Lloyd Wright in 1959, but in France, Le Corbusier, the builder of the controversial Chapel of Ronchamp, was making plans for the Olivetti Center near Milan and the hospital in Venice, both projects left unfinished since he died suddenly of a heart-attack in 1965. In 1960 Ludwig Mies Van der Rohe and Philip Johnson finished the Seagram building in New York and Richard Rodgers and Renzo Piano were about to embark on the Pompidou Center for Art and Culture in Paris. And suddenly, as from nowhere came the "far-out" Fritz Hundertwasser who remodeled some old facades in Vienna with most unusual results, not unlike, the unfinished Cathedral of Barcelona by Gaudi.

Especially as of the 1960s another positive phenomenon is most apparent, the emergence of the women artists, in music as well as the visual arts. We should not forget that Peggy Guggenheim had put on a Women's Art show as early as '45. However "One of the greatest effects of the women's movement is the unleashing of women's creativity in a great wave that is only the beginning" as Betty Friedan asserts. Of course we always had women artists; in music we have only to think on Fanny Mendelssohn, Amy Beach, and in painting there are Mary Cassatt or Georgia O'Keeffe, but they had always been the exception, rather than the norm.

Now the list, though not yet very long, is growing. In the visual arts most active are Louise Nevelson, Helen Frankenthaler, Françoise Gilot, Louise Bourgeois, Jennifer Bartlett, Elaine de Kooning. In music the most visible of the younger generation are Joan Tower, Barbara Kolb and Ellen Taaffe Zwilich, to name only three. Also in the pop field are many gifted women, some even reaching out into the art music world as a Lauri Anderson. Not to forget the many women who have made a name for themselves in the crowded music field as have Margareth Hillis, Leotyne Price, Beverly Sills and lest we omit there is Nadia Boulanger, the grande dame of Paris under whom most Americans went to study their craft— among them Bernstein and Copland.

State of the Art

A common complaint nowadays is: "I hate modem classical music. It always sounds so angry." And in fact many times it does. Are we, as some historians suggested, in the Age of Anger? Another simplistic observation we can hear is: "it looks so simple and dumb, anyone can do it." Perhaps. Gurdon Woods' words do have meaning when he said: "Art is idea. It is not enough to draw, to paint, and to sculpt. An artist should be able to think." And Miriam Shapiro said it in even simpler terms: "My God, as an artist I was given the right to do it as I wanted…"

So we are back at the age-old question "What is art." Maybe art is as simple as life. The way John Cage had it, and said so eloquently: "When we separate music from life what we get is art. With contemporary music, if it is actually contemporary, we have no time to make that separation, and so contemporary music is not so much art as it is life."

Art should have that sense of magic, that feeling of enchantment, that perception of awe, that has been so missing in our daily lives. When we get a certain happiness from it, when it brings us laughter or moves us to tears, then art has made its mark. Art should be like a flower, or a tree. It should be such that, when we don't have it, we miss it. It is like a person. Art and music are only meaningful when we can compare it to something positive. Nowadays we reject even the positive and the meaningful in art. Too often it is the ugly, negative, repulsive and perverse which draws attention, especially from museum curators and critics.

The arts should be clear, free, beautiful as a jewel, like something that we cannot do without. Trees once again can help us see who we are. People and trees have something in common. Trees are taller than anything growing—grasses, bushes, moss, etc. man is taller then most animals; birds, raccoons, beavers, snakes, worms or insects. Both man and trees are vertical and make the link between heaven and earth. A tree pushes its leaves into the heavens, whereas man reaches the heavens with his/her spirit. Only the feet keep us on the ground. Trees have yet a stronger visual polarity between heaven and earth—the roots—they are not only at ground level but actually penetrating it and anchoring the tree. But we are more than trees, we are free and art is more than nature.

Maybe if we had just listened to the words of C. P. E. Bach, J. S. Bach's second son, those may have been sufficient to explain what good music is; "I believe" he said, "that music must first and foremost stir the heart."

♪ Featured Music

Edgard Varèse (1883-1965), *Poème électronique* (1958)
At the age of thirty-two Varèse made a supposedly short visit to the New World, but he ended up staying and marrying here. This became like a symbolic complete break with his European past, as he often asserted.

In his earlier work, especially Ameriques (1921), he had to use existing instruments for the sounds he wanted to produce and often complained that "our musical alphabet must be enriched. We also need new instruments very badly..." His wish did not come true until the late '50's (by then he was 75) and finally he was able to compose his "Poème électronique" exclusively with artificial sound sources. Unfortunately it cannot be "performed" again, since it was 'fixed' on audiotape, in a studio, under his supervision. No conventional instrument is used and basically no "conventional music" is heard, only series of noises. The relatively short work of eight minutes, was heard within the Pavilion of the Philips Radio Corporation at the 1958 Brussels Worlds Fair. The composer worked with the equally controversial architect, Le Corbusier, who projected on the walls some photographs and paintings while the music was heard from 425 speakers placed all over the interior of the Pavilion.

The work falls in two sections, each introduced by cathedral-type of bells and ending with sirens. Symbolizing a drifting from peace to war? Especially in the second half, we hear snatches of a solo voice, choir and organ.

The first section (2:36)

Cathedral bell. Woodblocks. Siren. Fast taps. High piercing sound. Pause. Bongo. Grating noises. Duck squawks. Three times a three-note group. Sustained low notes with grating noises. Sirens. Squawks. Three=note. 2-second pause.
Squawks. Chirps. Honks. Machine noises. Sirens Tap

Second section (5:29)

Cathedral bell. Sustained tones. Bongo. High, sustained tone. Low tone with crescendo. Rhythmic noises. Female Voice. 4-second pause. Soft voice continues.

Suddenly louder. Rhythmic noises with voice. Animal noises, scraping, shuffling, vocal sounds, Decrescendo. 7-second pause.

Sustained tones, getting louder then softer. Rhythmic percussive sounds. High tones, getting louder. Airplane rumble. Chimes. Clanging sound. Female voice. Male choir.

Organ splashes. High taps. Organ sound again. Two times three-note group. Rumbling noises. Sirens.

Varese was unquestionably a very innovative composer, who in many ways was born too early since only towards the very end of his life could he find the sounds he was looking for. At first he had acoustical instruments do imitations of airplanes, animal noises and other unusual sounds. With the invention of the synthesizer most of these sounds were built-in. Varese had the habit of giving his pieces scientific names; Ionisations, Density 21.5', octandre etc. Without a doubt his influence was enormous, especially on john Cage, Milton Babbitt and many others who never dared tread where Varese had been.

Krzysztof Penderecki (1933-) *Threnody: To The Victims of Hiroshima* **(1960)**
Penderecki was one of a group of avant-garde composers emerging after the Stalinist revolt in Poland in 1956. The experimentations always had been suppressed by the Soviet Union, and now the Polish government encouraged the new cultural expression in films, painting, theatre, and music. The best known of the Polish composers is unquestionably Penderecki. The human suffering he saw as a young boy were expressed in such works as Dies Irae (1967), for the victims of Auschwitz; the St. Luke Passion (1965) depicts the suffering of Calvary in the most vivid and dramatic way. The Passion won universal acclaim from the Church, from the public as well as the critics, despite the uncompromising controversial techniques used in the score.

Just as Varèse before him, he gets some novel sounds out of the chorus (hissing, laughter, shouting, whistling) and instruments (clusters, glissandos, noise-like and percussive effects). The strings are often tapped or played beyond the "bridge" producing irritating and grating sounds. "Penderecki is Europe's most impressive new voice in modem music," reported Time Magazine in 1963, after a performance of the Passion in Venice's San Giorgio Church.

His Threnody, or song of mourning, is a very intense work, and although relatively short (8:57), almost intolerably harsh and irritating. There is no feeling of rhythm or beat of any kind and only once, at 2:27, is there any sense of a definite pitch. Threnody starts with a shrill sustained cluster, suddenly dropping off in intensity. After a siren-like sound, there is a brief pause. The low, sustained cluster grows in intensity and grows unbearably loud and piercing. Then there is a long decrescendo ending in a long 10-second pause. Pizzicatos, blips, and taps, sustained clusters lead again to a brief silence. Far away there is the rumble of jet-like roar. Silence again. Even without the context of Hiroshima, the work makes a frightening impression.

Igor Stravinskk(1882-1971), *In Memoriam Dylan Thomas* **(1954)**
Somewhere around 1952, Stravinsky's style started showing signs of change. There was a renewed interest in contrapuntal writing and his beginning use of a strict serial technique. The latter was most surprising, especially since he had criticized this procedure as being too cerebral, appealing to the intellect rather than to the heart. Eventually Stravinsky adapted that system in its entirety in later compositions, especially in Canticurn Sacrum, a work dedicated to the city of Venice.

In Memoriam Dylan Thomas was painful to write for Stravinsky, as Dylan Thomas was en route to live with Stravinsky, while he was to collaborate in a film of the Odyssey with the English producer Michael Powell. Then in New York, where he was scheduled to do poetry readings, Dylan Thomas suddenly died.

Stravinsky's choice from the poems of Dylan Thomas, "do not go gentle into that night... Good men... rage, rage against the dying of the light." is Thomas' best known poem, a desperate outcry at the approach of death. All of the music is derived from the first five notes, which he takes through different devices of inversions, backwards, upside down, mirror and other strict serial permutations. The trombone choir is always relieved by the string quartet, with the same music but twice as slow. The tenor repeats four times the "Rage, rage" music, more agitated and stringent, while the sting interlude is heard six times. Interesting enough the antiphonal use of the trombone choir and the strings is a also used in the aforementioned Canticum Sacrum for St. Mark's in Venice, which he was composing at the same time.

Just like that other genius of our century, Picasso, Stravinsky will also change styles even between two works that are chronologically adjacent. Both Picasso and Stravinsky were able to integrate all contemporary styles within their own work without losing their own identity. Unquestionably Stravinsky's music as of the early 1950s becomes more severe and austere, without ever restricting his multifaceted imagination.

Stravinsky's music was always a subject of controversy among musicians and listeners, nevertheless few reached his technical accomplishments or have shown such mastery in fashioning such an endless variety of varicolored styles and genres. He is admittedly one of the towering figures of the 20th century.

Philip Glass (1937-), *Glasspieces* **(1983)**
All minimalist music tend to sound the same, and that is the whole idea. However among the leading protagonists of minimalism, Philip Glass seems to stand out. Glass incorporated many influences in his music, not the least from Ravi Shankar, India's foremost sitar player and the music of India, and moreover his encounters with the North African Arab music in Morocco. Since the mid-seventies Glass has concentrated on music for the stage, and his first real success came with his opera "Einstein on the Beach" (1975). His opera "The Voyage" (1992), in commemoration of Columbus' landing in the Bahamas, was given six sold-out performances at the Metropolitan Opera in New York City. No small feat.

Another strong influence was the music and teachings of John Cage, whose influence upon the music in the 20th century was quite considerable. But unlike Cage's music, the minimalist's music is very controlled, even though changes in the melody and rhythm remain imperceptible and trance-like. Most interesting is that some rock groups often borrowed ideas from the minimalists, most notably Pink Floyd and the Tangerine group. Just as much as jazz and rock musicians, most minimalists perform their own music, with their own ensemble. Bach, Handel, Mozart and all the old masters had been doing that all along.

By minimalist standards this is a rather short piece. Most minimalist music can go on for hours, almost like chants or mantras of the Eastern religions. Because of its repetitious character, its stripped-down diatonicism, the widespread use of scale passages and other tonal quotations, all combined reestablishes the feel of the traditional tonal stability. This is a remarkable return to the repossession of the tonal center that was so rudely disposed of at the beginning of the century. Most composers grew up in a climate of dissonance and atonality, and rediscovering tonality was almost a discovery of something new. The idea is to construct a new image, a new sound, rather than to revive the past.

Ellen Taaffe Zwilich (1939-), *Symphony No. 1* (1983)
Unquestionably Ellen Taaffe Zwilich has become the dean of the present-day American composers. Besides being an accomplished violinist, she has quite an impressive list of distinguished compositions and has been the recipient of many prestigious awards, including the Pulitzer Prize in music for her Symphony No. 1 in three movements.

The symphony is laid out in a broadly scoped ABA form. The first section is an introduction, calm and serene, presenting three statements of a rising third motive, each accompanied by a quickening of the tempo. It is the growing seed for the more dramatic middle section of the movement. This time the tempo is much quicker, but at the same time with less fluctuations as before. The thematic configuration of the thirds is spread out to larger intervals, thereby increasing the tension and intensifying the dramatic effect, especially since there are some sharp dissonant clashes. Eventually a chime announces the dissipation of the energy and the chord slowly dies away, while three chimes signal the beginning of the coda. A two-note motive continues rocking over a quiet trombone chord. One more time the oboe wails out the motive, and soon a warm, intense melody replies in the cellos. The first movement evaporates quietly with a peaceful gesture.

A most interesting work by Ellen Taaffe Zwilich is the Concerto Grosso 1985 which "quotes" a G. F. Handel Sonata for Violin and Continuo while interspersing it freely with her own music that use dissonances in a twentieth-century manner.

John Corigliano (1938-), *Symphony #1 (1990)*
As mentioned before one of the features of post-1960 music are the quotations within the music. Even in the visual arts we have the collages—usually newspapers, pieces of wood or cloth, as reminders or "souvenirs" of an event or person. It was mostly used by the early cubists and Dadaists.

The event that was the spark to Corgliano's symphony was the AIDS epidemic. Having lost some friends and seeing "The Quilt," a memorial tribute to each of the victims, made him want to memorialize them in music.

The symphony has three movements and en epilogue. Each movement has a certain person in mind. The Apologue speaks of a pianist-friend, the second, a Tarantella, an Italian dance, talks of an executive in the music industry, the third is a tribute to an amateur cellist with a lengthy Chaconne, a passacaglia-type set of variations. The Epilogue weaves the three movements as a quilt-like rug into a recapitulation of their dialogues. The music slowly fades away in memory lane.

The first movement, apologue, is cast in a large-scale ABA form. An Apologue is an allegorical narrative intended to convey a moral, according to Webster's Dictionary. The movement starts out as the subtitle suggests: Of Rage and Remembrance, with an ever-crescendoing unison string sound, responded with a highly charge electric bolt coming from the percussion. This is repeated three times with ever-increasing intensity and vehemence, in wild ferocity as the score demands. The pent-up anger reaches a peak topped by violins in their highest register. Gradually the violins release their frustration as we enter the B section of the movement. In the distance we hear a piano playing, Albeniz's Tango, a favorite piece of his friend. A long extended lyrical passage follows, fragmented with bits and pieces of the same Tango. Little by little a drumbeat starts being heard, its accelerando becoming more insistent culminating in a recapitulation. (A)

By this time the entire orchestra joins in an increasing forte, in near-hysteria emphatically playing a deafening dissonant chord. Mercifully they finally let go, its energy exhausted. Some previous themes are recapitulated and the piano brings a final Tango-salute to a desolate high A in the orchestra.

The movement is very emotional and leaves one exhausted and drained. Most previous composers, be it Beethoven, Berlioz or Wagner, will, even in their most somber and tenebrous pieces, bring a spark of hope and confidence, but this symphony never lifts its gloomy head of bittersweet nostalgia of the tension of anger and memory. Obviously the toll of his loss to the Aids epidemic was inconsolable and the music is and eloquent, albeit somber and poignant tribute to his friends and to all who lost loved ones to this scourge.

And still we have the vexing question "What Is Art?" Is it as John Cage so eloquently states: "When we separate music from life what we get is art. With contemporary music, when it is actually contemporary, we have no time to make that separation, and so contemporary music is not so much art as it is life."

Nevertheless contemporary art and music is difficult to understand and very often people turn away from it disgusted or disappointed. And yet, only when it is full of magic is art good, is music good, is painting good, is literature good, is poetry good is a movie good. When we find a certain happiness, when we are moved to laughter or to tears, when it moves us from within is art, no matter when it was done, no matter by whom.

Art must be like a flower or a tree. It must such that we miss it when it is not there. It is like a person. When we can compare to a flower, a tree or a person. Then and only then can we speak of good art. Unfortunately all art seems to be rejected—if it is beautiful or not, positive or not, and very often the ugly, the negative, the repulsive and even the perverse has a chance—at least by the museum curators or the music critics.

The State of music since the 1980s

- The use of the twelve-tone system has dropped considerably (ever since 1970s)
- Serialism (especially in France): use of techniques that systematize pitches, Rhythm, and even dynamics and tone color. Most prominent exponent Pierre Boulez, Olivier Messiaen and others.
- Aleatory music: random chance of choosing pitch, tone color, and rhythm. Leaves great freedom to the performer who can pick, choose and arrange.
- Minimalist music: rhythmically uniform and motoric, with obstinate repetitions of short melodic phrases, resulting in clear tonality. Needs some sort of visual background.
- Collage: collage effect with quotations of inserting traditional materials into another fabric.
- Experimental use of unusual sounds (prepared piano, brake drums, thunder sheets, Chains, changing turntable speeds, etc.) John Cage was the great innovator.

Women Composers

One of the greatest effects off the women's movement is the unleashing of women's creativity in a great wave that is only the beginning.
                                                                    —Betty Friedan

Ironically, while much history remains unknown concerning women composers, the first composer scholars do know by name is a woman, Hildegard von Bingen. Besides being a noted composer, she was also an abbess, mystic, poet, and physician. What is known about her accurately reflects much of what is known and unknown about society itself. What society then valued is what was recorded and what is known.

Critics and artists suggest that since the arts (i.e., music) were male-dominated for centuries, it is almost impossible to truly understand and access "women's music." Almost, but *not quite impossible,* as this chapter will illustrate.

Since the early 1970's, feminism has dramatically altered women's fortunes, certainly within the United States, and more pertinently, within music. Women's increasing representation in higher education (e.g., students and educators) further broadens their inclusion within music's ranks. Nevertheless, long predating the Feminist Movement, fine examples occur of women boldly enduring ridicule and adversity to achieve sustained musical success.

Traditionally, women's struggles in music have mirrored those of women in society itself. Custom and mores limited their educational and professional options. Moreover, legally, until the twentieth century, women were universally considered merely as their fathers' or husbands' property, having no independent rights or privileges. While these legalities are largely eradicated in the United States and Europe, they still, unfortunately, exist elsewhere.

Within music's two basic divisions, performance and composition, women have fared better as performers than composers. For instance, noted composer Guillaume de Machaut (1300?-1377) lavishly praised Madame Peronne d'Armentières as the best singer (i.e., of either sex) that he had ever heard.

Hildegard von Bingen (1098-1179) is then the first entrée in a meager listing of female composers. Her aristocratic parents offered her to God by entering her at age right in Rupertsberg's Benedictine Monastery, along the Rhine near Frankfurt. Hildegard wrote numerous theological, physical science, and medical texts, while still pursuing poetry, letter writing, and composition. Her morality play *Ordo virtutum* contains nearly 80 vocal pieces, all dealing with the soul's struggle against the Devil's temptations. Illustrating her humorous style, each piece was sung by the nuns, except the piece for the Devil who had been denied the gift of song, it was sung by the monastic chaplain! This proved a wry commentary on the restrictions placed upon women within music.

In 1174 Pope Eugenius declared von Hildegard Bingen a true prophet. Interestingly, she practiced the medieval musical custom of equating the flute sound with God's presence, strings connoting the Soul, and bells representing rejoicing. Vocal lines were mostly either like Gregorian chants or initial attempts at polyphony in the prevailing Parisian School. Unfortunately, having retained little more than pitch, many of the pieces still require considerable redress. The group most responsible for reviving Hildegard von Bingen is Sequentia—the world's leading Medieval music ensemble. Their remarkable performances are formulated, after much painstaking research, from ancient codexes and manuscripts.

While Renaissance humanism flourished, opportunities for women declined. They could neither receive musical education nor perform in churches. Women fortunate enough to perform secularly worked gratis, while their male counterparts received salaries. Despite this compensation inequity, most female operatic roles were performed by male eunuchs. As the very words unknowingly suggest, "Renaissance humanism" was indeed limited to a Renaissance for Men. This severe sexism extended throughout the Baroque period as well.

Romanticism's genesis brought about a slow, but still welcome change regarding women's musical opportunities. The keys to this growing favor are found in political revolutions and the burgeoning popularity of the piano. While politics and technology might not be the most expedient factors, in this instance they sufficed quite effectively.

One of the first female composers to receive acknowledgment from the musical establishment (at least from Felix, her renowned musician brother) was the talented Fanny Mendelssohn. This faith in her musical talent was not share by her father (otherwise considered a social progressive) who penned her a well-intentioned, yet devastating letter consigning her musical interest and fervor to its "proper place." He adamantly stated that music is to remain "an ornament and never the basis of your existence." He advised, "Remain true to these sentiments and to this line of conduct; they are feminine, and only what is feminine is an ornament to your sex." Fortunately, following her marriage to the painter Wilhelm Hensel, she resumed her compositions, publishing them mostly under her brother's name. Felix's letters underscore his high evaluation of her acumen and musical ability. Eventually, she published four books of melodies under her own name. When in 1847 she suddenly died at age 42, within six months Felix died of grief from her passing.

Mendelssohn's contemporary was Clara Schumann, née Wieck. Her father, Friedrich, though a domineering parent, helped Clara become one of Europe's most acclaimed virtuoso pianists. Her concert tours always contained some of her own compositions. Her marriage to Robert Schumann created a difficult predicament of raising seven children, which curtailed both her performances and compositions. Being married to a supremely gifted composer, Clara doubted her own abilities. Yet, she resumed her career after Robert's untimely death.

Amy Beach was the first American woman receiving international praise. She was born, Amy Cheney, in 1867. This precocious only child of colonial dissenters gave her first piano recital at age seven, playing several of her own waltzes. Later, her husband, Dr. H. H. Beach, greatly encouraged Amy to pursue composition and concertizing. She wrote several major pieces for piano, orchestra, and choir, publishing them under the moniker "Mrs. H.H.A. Beach." After her husband's death, she concertized her own compositions in Germany. Critics enthusiastically acclaimed her, and audiences considered Amy an important American composer. Until her own death in 1944, at the age of 77, Amy remained one of America's leading talents of the early twentieth century.

Currently, the United States has several accomplished female composers. Three major talents—Libby Larsen, Joan Tower, and Ellen Taafe Zwilich—merit special attention. Although none is a household name, each produces a dominant force on the American concert stage.

Born in the Midwest, Libby Larson has been fascinated by the World of percussion. She wrote the highly successful *Concerto for Marimba,* a work performed by the Louisville Symphony Orchestra.

Joan Tower achieved national stature with her sparkling piece Sequoia. Her Fanfare for the Uncommon Woman (written in tribute to the uncommon woman who takes risks and seeks adventure) parallels Aaron Copland's own *Fanfare for the Common Man.* As a vehicle for her lectures, Tower tirelessly advocates contemporary music. In 1969 she founded the *Da capo Chamber Ensemble,* which tours throughout America and abroad.

The third and perhaps best known composer is Ellen Taaffe Zwilich. She became the first American woman to earn a Doctorate in Composition at Julliard. In 1983 her Symphony No. I received music's coveted Pulitzer Prize. She has since written a large amount of symphonic and chamber works. Zwilich insists that composing has nothing to do with gender, stating "music is about humanity." To critics who regard her music as very powerful, she questions if indeed women are understood. She wonders if feminine is synonymous with weak, soft, tender, and fragile?

As previously noted, women have always fared better (especially since the 1900s) as performers. The long list of eminent performers includes: Leontyne Price, Marion Anderson, Beverly Sills, Sara Caldwell, Ruth Crawford Seeger, Elisabeth Lutyens, Thea Musgrave, and many others active in opera, solo careers, etc.

Although men dominate vernacular music, women have powerfully impacted rock music. Women control their own careers by being lead singers, playing instruments, and composing their own music. Many names appear covering many styles; soul, funk, heavy metal, country, bluegrass, rock, folk, and Broadway. Leading artists include: Loretta Lynn, Madonna, Linda Ronstadt, Tina Turner, Diana Ross, Carole King, Joan Baez, Queen Latifah, and many more deserving recognition. Omissions are inherently endemic to even the most exhaustive of studies; they are not a reflection of a particular artist's talent. Hence, this work is mindful of its own oversights.

However, all of these twentieth-century composers are Americans. Where are the Europeans, South Americans, or any other peoples? Many of these countries possess influential women artists in the realm of painting, sculpture, poetry, architecture, drama, and musical performance, but not as composers? Why have women not surfaced as creative artists? Is there indeed a possible untried solution? Perhaps the answer lies in Georgia O'Keefe's remarks written at the turn of the century:

> *"One day I found myself saying to myself... I can't live where I want to... I can't go where I want to... I can't do what I want to. I can't even say what I want to. I decided I was a very stupid fool not to at least paint as I want to and say what I want to when I painted, as that seems to be the only thing I could do that didn't concern anybody but myself."*

References

Loesser, Arthur. *Men, Women, and Pianos: A Social History.* New York: Simon & Schuster, 1990.

Munro, Eleanor. *Originals: American Women Artists.* New York: Simon & Schuster, 1979.

Reich, Nancy. *Clara Schumann: The Artist and the Woman.* New York:

Werner, Eric. *Mendelssohn: A New Image of the Composer and His Age.* New York: Free Press, 1963.

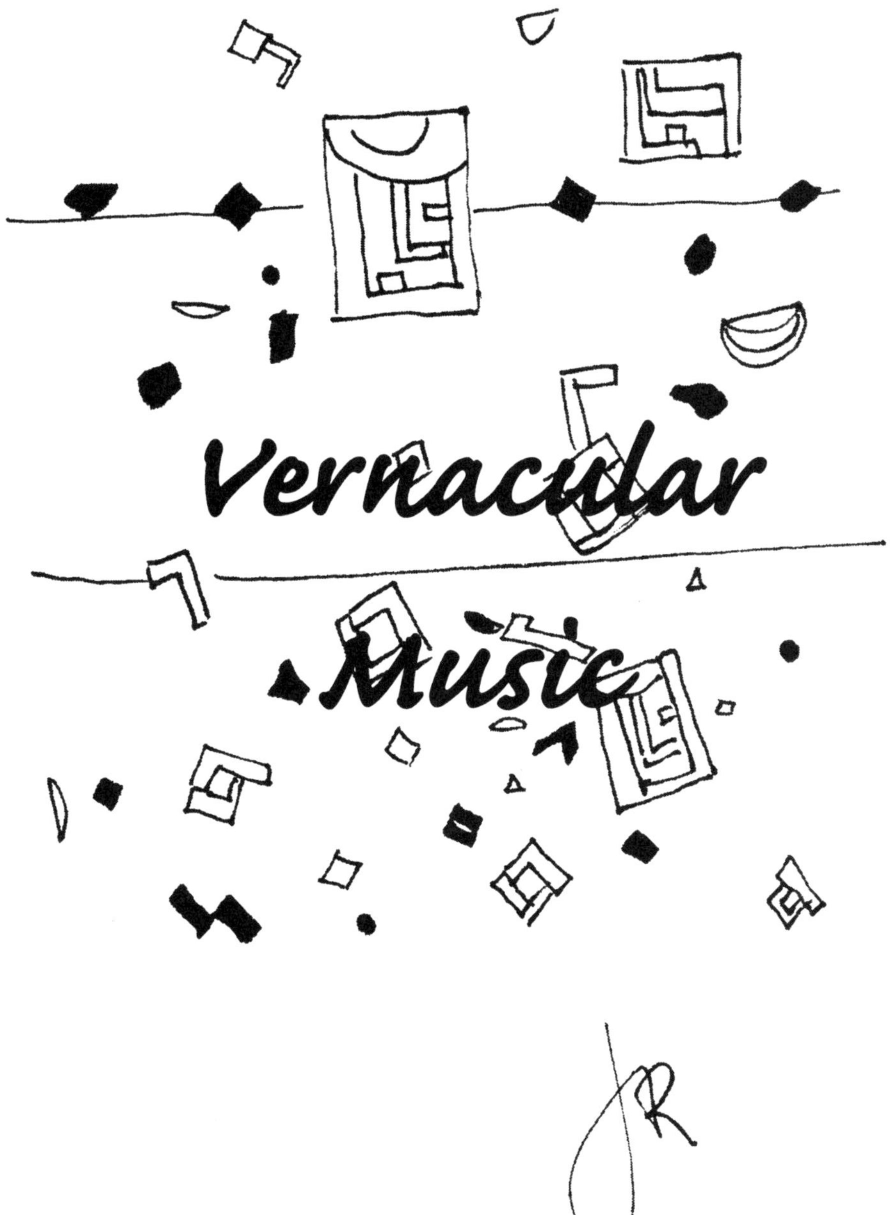
Vernacular
Music

*"The best and most perfect way that we have of expressing
a sweet concord of mind to each other is by music."*
—Jonathan Edwards

Jazz

Jazz is a birth child of the Southern United States, and of Louisiana specifically. The word jazz itself is a slang word with many meanings, but in music it means a new musical style that is rooted in the African-American community, that relies on improvisation and syncopated rhythms. The origins of jazz are obscure, but most definitely flowing from the *"call and answer"* songs as expressed by the slaves working in the fields picking cotton, husking corn, planting potatoes or by the chain-gang of those jailed. Another sources were the many "Negro Spirituals" as sung in the churches of the black communities. Unfortunately very little was captured on recordings before 1923 and none before 1917, when the Original Dixieland Band was first recorded.

Jazz has many styles: Dixieland, Blues, Swing, Bebop, Cool Jazz, Funky, Fusion, Jazz-Rock and lately Jazz Latin. Very early on, jazz made an enormous impact, especially on prominent composers such as Debussy, Ravel, Milhaud, Bernstein, Stravinsky and many, many others.

While it is true that the cradle stood in New Orleans, its consequent nurturing was accomplished in the north and Midwest, its appreciation was most fervent worldwide, especially Europe, with Paris at its center.

What is Jazz

The roots of jazz are a mixture of West African, American and European, although there are two dominant sources;

1.   The African slaves, mostly from the areas that include Nigeria, Ghana, and some other West African nations, where there is still a great emphasis put on improvisation; percussion and complex cross rhythms. Most important is the *"call and response"* feature coming from the same sources. The leader sings a phrase, which is responded by the larger group. This technique is still used by preachers and political leaders; e.g. Martin Luther King. In music, the whole group answers a solo instrument's call. A feature especially strong in "swing."

Other sources from the African-American community were the gospel hymns and spirituals, and also dances like the cakewalk, black bottom, juba, shimmy and turkey trot. Although very little has been preserved, as nothing was written down, many scholars believe that there must still be a great resemblance to the earlier jazz music

2.   From the white community, jazz musicians borrowed harmony as was commonly heard in hymns, popular songs, marches, and piano music and dance music.

Since virtually every city or village had a band playing for parades, carnivals, political rallies, those bands—either black or white—had an enormous influence upon the jazz bands: same instruments (trumpet, trombone, tuba, and clarinet, and drums) similar harmony and forms.   ·

Thus the combination of African and American elements was the backbone of early jazz.

Ragtime is the "jazz" music of the 1890s. Most of the practitioners were African-Americans who played in saloons and dance halls. The ragtime music, ordinarily for the piano, was based on march music. The left hand, with a steady "oo,-pah: accompaniment, supports the highly syncopated melody of the right hand. The form is simply AA-BB-CC-DD-EE, similar to the marches. The steady beat, the syncopated melody was readily adapted by jazz musicians.

The "King of Ragtime" was unquestionably Scott Joplin (1868-1917). The son of a former slave, Joplin was educated on "classical" music. He even wrote a ballet and two operas, but his fame rests in the piano rags, especially *Maple Leaf Rag*, named after the saloon in Sedalia, MI. It was published in 1899. In 1909 he moved to New York City. He desperately tried to have his opera, *Treemonisha*, performed in 1915, but without success. That failure undermined his already frail health and after a long stay at the hospital he died in 1917.

Blues

The origin of the blues is uncertain. The blues were first heard in the fields of the South; Mississippi, South and North Carolina, Georgia, and Tennessee. Most of the lyrics speak of unrequited love, betrayal and inexpressible loneliness. Although not all blues are sad, most have a strong feeling of melancholy. Some typical African characteristics are; the "blue" notes, micro tonal pitch inflections on the third, fifth and seventh degree of the major scale; the so-called *"call and response"*; the falsetto break of the singer's voice, adding to its imitation of sobbing; and the imitation of idioms by the voice of instruments, especially the guitar and brass.

Characteristic of the blues are also the harmonic structure. Blues ordinarily have twelve measures, equally divided in three measures at a time. The chords used are tonic (I) the subdominant (IV) and the dominant (V) of the given scale

> Schematically it looks like:
>
> Phrase 1 (measures 1-4) I-I-I-I: *I was with you baby when you did not have a dime*
>
> Phrase 2 (measures 5-8) IV-IV-I-I: *I was with you baby when you did not have a dime.*
>
> Phrase 3 (measures 9-12) V-IV-I-I: *Now since you got plenty money you have throw'd your good gal down.*
>
> The words and music *Lost Your Head Blues* (19260 by Bessie Smith. The singer's melody only occupies two measures, the other two measures are a reply to the "call" of the singer by a cornet. In the second phrase the melody to the same words has slight variant, also replied to. Same goes for the third phrase and once again the cornet replies with an improvised answer.

All jazz is inherently rooted in the blues. If the blues were nurtured in the South, it was the North that brought it to maturity. Cities like Chicago, Kansas City, and New York made the blues into a popular item of entertainment. Bessie Smith was the first consummate blues singer and her recordings and personal appearances dominated the 1920s. Her *Mama's got the Blues* became the supreme model of the vocal blues style. In the instrumental field it was Louis Armstrong who perfected the blues to a true art form. Blues did not always have lyrics and the piano-blues were often called *Boogie-woogie*, bright in mood and driven by a fast-moving ostinato bass. Who will ever top *Rhapsody in Blue* by Gershwin?

Dixieland

While most musicians were playing blues, some developed an original jazz style, called Dixieland, around the turn of the century. New Orleans became the center to such greats as Ferdinand "Jelly Roll" Morton, Joseph "King" Oliver and Louis Armstrong. Their music was heard everywhere at picnics, parades or dance halls. The African-American community also played music on the way to and from the cemetery, slow and solemn at first, while on the way back, knowing that the deceased was in a better place, the music turned to happier rhythms and tunes. Typically those groups were small, five to eight instrumentalists. The melody line players (cornet, trumpet, clarinet and trombone) were supported by the rhythm section playing the chords (guitar, banjo, or piano) and the bass line was taken by the plucked bass or tuba. The music was often based on hymns, marches, or popular tunes, often blues as well. *When the Saints Go Marching In* was a typical tune of those days. The chorus played the tune at the beginning and the end, and in between different improvised solos were featured, at times unaccompanied, called breaks. At the end the there even was a coda, called a *Tag*. Most often the trumpeter was the leader playing improvised variations to the tune, while above the clarinet wove a faster moving counter melody, while the trombone played some sort of bass line to it. The music typically divides into nine 12-bar choruses, chorus 1, 5 and 9 taken by the collective improvisation by all the instruments, the others having improvised solos.

Louis Armstrong was the undisputed master of the New Orleans Style or Dixieland. Through changes of rhythm and pitch, he transformed ordinary tunes into extraordinary solos, playing even unheard of high notes on his instrument. Also his singing of nonsense syllables, scat singing as it was called, set the standard conveying the same jazz feel as the trumpet.

Swing

In the 1920s yet an another style developed, swing, flourishing to the end of Word War 11. Big bands were the vehicle as it was mainly aimed at large ballrooms that had proliferated around the country. Hundreds of big bands, both black and white, carried big names, including: Duke Ellington, Count Basie, Glenn Miller, Tommy Dorsey, and Benny Goodman, Billie Holiday, Ella Fitzgerald, Frank Sinatra and many others.

Jazz, which had been associated with bars, brothels, and burlesque establishments, became suddenly respectable music. In 1938 jazz made it all the way to the venerable Carnegie Hall in New York City with Benny Goodman's historic jazz concert, with Duke Ellington's not far behind.

The jazz orchestra also grew in size, no longer the small New Orleans band, most orchestras now numbered fourteen or more members. Improvisation with such a large group became unwieldy and most often the "arranger" became a sought after profession. Solos were shorter and the main melodies were often interjected with short, repeated passages called *riffs*. The saxophones became the most important solo instruments, together with the percussion. The legendary Gene Krupa played some spectacular solos on his drum set.

In swing the second and fourth beats were stressed adding to the excitement of the already rich and varied sounds of the group. But as always the 12-bar was still the underlaying form. At times popular songs were used and occasionally a 32-bar principle applied. Such compositions resorted to the three-part classical model of A-A-B-A, each having 8-bar phrases and called a chorus. Most pieces had a total of four choruses, resulting in 128 measures, sometimes with an 8 measure introduction.

The sound of the Big Band was polished, smooth, swinging and inherently singable. Edward "Duke" Ellington (1899-1974) was the leading composer, arranger and conductor of the Swing Ear. His works are rich in harmony, more varied in form than most and his success here and abroad assured his place among the greats of swing.

Bebop

Because swing became more and more commercialized, arranged and orchestrated as its 'classical' counterpart, the essential element of jazz, improvisation, became more and more obsolete. Bebop in many ways was a rebellion to this development. Their sophisticated harmony, and unpredictable rhythms were the province of the "in" group, who differentiated themselves by their dress, goatees and hip language. That new breed could count on trumpeter Dizzy Gillespie, Theloneus Monk, and saxophonist Charlie "Bird" Parker. Their combos were again smaller, mainly a saxophone, trumpet, and a piano, bass and drums. The piano was no longer just a beat keeper, but payed some complex chord structures at irregular intervals, while the right hand played some intricate melodies and rapid passages often based on church modes or artificial scales. The abss drum also left its traditional role and occasionally dropped some *"bombs"* instead of just stomping out beats. The bebop musician was still using the 12-bar blues as a launching pad, although their forte was the free improvisation on newly composed tunes.

Charlie "Bird" Parker was the towering figure of the bebop scene and the most gifted improviser of that style. With his amazing virtuosity on the saxophone he was able to control recklessly fast tempi, and his lightning-swift improvisations of jagged, dry and angular melodies.

Cool Jazz

Very related to bebop is a jazz style that appeared in the early 1950s. It was called *Cool Jazz*, in contrast to the "Hot Jazz" of its predecessor. Once again the arranger was needed, as most of the music tended to stem from Classical" music, most notably Baroque masters, especially Bach. Their music was intended for the listener, not the dance hall. Their music was rather subdued, almost like chamber music and often featured instruments not normally associated with jazz, such as the flute, violin, French horn—all resulting in a smooth, mellow, and exquisitely blended sound of high sophistication. Personalities connected with cool jazz were Miles Davis, Dave Brubeck, and John Coltrane. The Modern Jazz Quartet set the place of the new style, experimenting with odd meters (5/4 or 7/4). Eventually this style expanded to *Free Jazz*, a totally free-wheeling style that was no longer beholden to the 12-bar blues, or prefabricated harmonies. Ornette Coleman became the leader of the avant-garde style. Everyone was 'free' to do what they felt of doing, and as in bebop the bass and percussion were given more melodic and rhythmic freedom. John Coltrane (1926- 19670) was the leading exponent of Free Jazz, until his untimely death at the age of forty. Most interesting was his use of drones and unusual scales that sprouted from his interest in Indian and Arabian music.

Funky

Some purest jazz musicians became more and more disenchanted with the direction of jazz. They believed that jazz had lost its roots and the original premise. They used gospel music with its simpler harmonic structure and greater rhythmic simplicity—which got to be known as "soul." Artists who were influential in the funky style were Horace Silver, and Art Blakey, besides Larry Graham, Marvin Gay and Herbie Hancock.

Fusion

The latest development in jazz is a commingling of jazz with rock styles, pop and occasionally Latin and classical music. There is an exhausting long list of names starting with Miles Davis, Herbie Hancock, Keith Jarrett, Chick Correa, Pat Metheny, Marian McPartland, and many more. Many new term bandied about: Third Stream, a synthesis of jazz and Latin; the fusion of Caribbean, and Brazilian rhythms, Bluegrass jazz with David Grisman: and rap jazz as performed, by Urbanator, Herbie Hancock and Muckhead.

Labeling of jazz musicians is like trying to categorize all the fish in the ocean. Many jazz musicians defy any labeling, starting out as bebop musicians, then flirting with Cool Jazz, and eventually moving on to Fusion, or some other ill-defined jazz style. This would easily describe Miles Davis, for instance. But he is by no means a solitary figure,: Max Roach, Sean Kenton, all defy grouping because so many of the jazz greats continue growing, continue to experiment, and continue to move on.

Rock Music

Post World War II, a new day dawned in pop music which would expand its infinite variety even further. First termed rock and roll, it was later simply called *rock*. Its resolute presence requires exploration.

Rock history divides into three phases;

1. *Rhythm and Blues* (R&B) originated in the early 1950s, incorporated blues with a stronger beat and the electric guitar as the center. Chuck Berry was the leading proponent. Eventually, R&B evolved into an early style of rock, wherein Elvis Presley was the crowned King by his large teenage following.

2. The first "English Invasion" began in 1964. The Beatles (soon joined by the Rolling Stones, Dave Clark Five, Byrds, Doors, etc.) literally transformed the American scene. By 1970 this musical transformation turned into musical devastation when the Beatles announced their dissolution, and drug overdoses claimed the lives of Jimmy Hendrix and Janis Joplin. A rebirth happened with Emerson, Lake and Palmer performing "Classical Rock" i.e. using classical music as a canvas to work from.

3. A myriad of new forces coalesced in the 1980s. A second "English Invasion" brought the Culture Club, The Police, and Eurhythmics. Their style, different from the Beatles, increasingly utilized the modern technology with computers and synthesizers. Heavy Metal became in vogue, especially among adolescents. Meanwhile black folks favored Rap.

Initially, rock began similar to jazz—with a small band composed of two electric guitars (one lead and the other rhythm) electric bass, percussion, and keyboard. The latter was promptly replaced by a synthesizer. Most of the "singing" sounded closer to shouts, screams, and wailing—interjected with nonsensical syllables (yeah, yeah, yeah) in sharp contrast with the crooning of the previous Swing Ear, as exemplified by Frank Sinatra. Rock rhythm, driven by a powerful beat, maintained a quick tempo strongly accented on the downbeat. Although frequently patterned after the 12-bar or even the 32-bar of the popular music arrangements, many rock musicians utilized irregular phrasing with short melodic repetitions. The harmonic background was often strewn with simple chords, occasionally even relying on a two chord pattern as in John Lennon and Paul McCartney's Eleanor Rigby.

Rock and dancing are kindred spirits. In the early 60s most rock music was improvisational—anything goes over a powerful beat. In the 70s people danced in discotheques to the omnipresent hustle, while line dancing revived. In the 80s, *breakdancing* (combining dancing with gymnastics) was perpetuated by the film *Flashdance*.

What is Rock music?

During the early 50s some enthusiasts considered rock as the new dawn of popular music; others perceived it as the thrashing of jazz. In *"The Story Of Rock"* Carl Belz astutely equates rock with folk art. He reasoned that rock originated from youth-oriented pop-music, a mishmash of jazz, pop, and country music. These repercussions echoed in art and politics. Its youthful vitality extended into the visual arts, exemplified by the emergence of Andy Warhol and others. During the term of President Kennedy and First Lady Jackie, commonly termed *Camelot* years, all responded to the zest, freshness and vibrancy of the changing social milieu. The younger generation's lifestyle differed radically from the older generation's culture. Rock, symbolizing this concept nearly perfectly, was accepted almost unanimously and instantly.

Many divergent musicians strongly influenced popular music. The dynamic power of the following musicians are exemplary: Scott Joplin, Louis Armstrong, Bessie Smith, Duke Ellington, Glenn Miller, Benny Goodman to name just a few. However, the steadfast invincibility of strength and duration on impact is shared by only two entities—Elvis Presley and the Beatles. Both their originality and inimitable style was a formula for longevity and continuity. Consequently, many imitators plugged into that winning current, to varying degrees of success. True, Elvis did not write the music he performed; but his charisma and compelling stage presence created an utterly unique musical persona. He even earned the acknowledged respect and awe of the Beatles. Reciprocally, Elvis was a member of this mutual admiration society. He realized the while he was the King, it was the Beatles who owned claim to the *Magical Kingdom*.

Elvis Presley

Born impoverished in Tupelo, MS, Elvis always enjoyed singing. Not until he was sixteen, however, did his unique talent of singing, clothing, and coiffure capture attention. In 1953, for his mother's birthday, Elvis whimsically made a recording which served inadvertently to inaugurate a brilliant career. His vocal style, first called *rock-a-billy*, after Bill Haley and the Comets, soon achieved world-wide appeal. Elvis quickly became also known as the "Hillbilly Cat, and his Blue Moon Boy's." By the age of nineteen, Elvis was 1954s hottest pop-music personality.

After several TV appearances, the press began asking if Elvis was merely a fad or signaled a new direction in entertainment. Noted critic Jack Gould pondered," Is he a good influence? Or bad? Is he dangerous?" The answer continued being debated after Elvis' return to U.S. films, recordings, and concerts, following his two-year Army stint. Though momentarily eclipsed by the Beatles' fame, he enjoyed a successful 1968 comeback. Henceforth, Elvis became established "superstar" becoming even more celebrated following his premature death. Unfortunately, his destructive lifestyle and excessive use of medications for insomnia, lupus, and severe kidney problems, took their toll. On August 16, 1977, Elvis died. Yet, even Variety declared,: Elvis Dead;: Good career Move." As proof, his lasting influence extends to Elvis Costello, and iceskater Elvis Stolerynko.

Presley's most successful recordings include: *Heartbreak Motel, Hound Dog, and Love me tender.* However, through the magic of computerized technology we can expect Elvis to continue appearing, much as Humphrey Bogart enhances televion Cola commercials.

Long live the King.

The Beatles

It is almost impossible to overestimate the Beatles' force and influence upon music's culture during the 1960s. After an acclaimed rise to fame in England and Germany, the Beatles were introduced to American audiences Sunday, February 9, 1964, on the *Ed Sullivan Show*. There were over fifty thousand requests for a theater that seated only seven hundred. The audience screams, lasting for over five minutes, heralded the start of Beatlemania. Even Dr. Joyce Brothers(nationally know psychological guru) was asked to analyze the ramifications of the Beatles' impact upon American society, The Beatles, were, are, and ever shall be.

Emulating Elvis, the Beatles, eventually parlayed their triumphs into the movies. Their feature films—*A Hard Day's Night, Help!, Magical Mystery Tour*—further established the Beatles' bona fide legitimacy. With each film or concert, their reputation, status, and audience size swelled exponentially. In 1965 the Beatles pointedly met Elvis, then residing in Los Angeles. Although they discussed a joint venture, it never materialized. Somehow, Elvis and the Beatles were destined to be jointly crowned by public acclamation and record sales of rock's two important forces.

During their annual world tour in 1966, the Beatles (especially John Lennon) became embroiled in a nasty controversy. During an interview, Lennon claimed that the Beatles were more popular than Jesus Christ. This remark proved unsettling and the sales of records, memorabilia, radio promotions, and concert plummeted, especially in the United States. 1966 marked their last tour as a group. By 1968 they had officially split.

On December 8, 1980, a young man, Mark Chapman, fatally shot John Lennon, thereby forever ending the magic of the Beatles. This event's impact is realized by the fact that age-appropriate Americans most often remember their own whereabouts upon hearing about: the attack on Pearl Harbor, John Kennedy's assassination, and John Lennon's demise.

For ten years the Beatles dominated the music field—both within the United States and internationally. Their universal appeal was unprecedented. *I want to hold your hand* remains the biggest selling single record of all time.

Woodstock

August 5, 1969, marked an event that forever changed how elders looked upon their offspring. This event personified the long-simmering societal protest, especially among the under thirty generation. This event, Woodstock, became an icon for peace, revolution, and sentiment against racism, hatred, sexism, poverty, and especially the Vietnam War. It also symbolized the temporary end of the growth and interest in rock.

Soon, however, some badly needed new blood was transfused into the ailing rock scene. The mid 1970s saw disco, a dance craze that swept from Paris across to the States. Eventually, disco entrenched itself via the enormously successful Saturday Night fever, featuring John Travolta. Yet, as the 1970s ended, so did disco—until its reappearance in another guise on MTV.

MTV, or Music Television, is now the vehicle of choice for popular music's dissemination. Soon after its inception, MTV spawned a new phenomenon, Michael Jackson. Though Jackson and his brothers previously enjoyed a credible musical career, that success was eclipsed by Michael and his innovative music videos. As proof, his *Thriller* sold over forty million copies in one year, becoming the best-selling record album of all time. In 1985, Michael Jackson engineered the stalwart video and light production of Epcot/Disney World in Orlando, Florida. During 1990, he signed a multimillion dollar deal with Sony, as their artistic consultant for filming and producing videos. He swiftly became a mega-star.

Also during this decade, Madonna epitomized the pioneering, female superstar. Almost since inception, Madonna stiffed controversy with her lyrics, appearance, and suggestive dancing. Her second album, *Like a Virgin*, and her starring role in *Desperately Seeking Susan*, mercurially positioned her in the international limelight. In 1989 Madonna's highly successful album, *Like a Payer* was followed by a leading role in *Dick Tracy*, a film with Warren Beatty. Then she starred as Evita Peron in the film of the same name. Her most controversial video, *Justify My Love*, was even banned by the usually lenient MTV. Her growing infamy steadily increased her net worth.

Fortunately, besides being musically successful, she possesses an impressive business acumen. In 1990 alone, the IRS claimed she owed an estimated $39 million dollars from earnings on over a half-billion dollars via the entertainment giant Time Warner.

In the late 1970s *Punk* emerged as a reaction against the establishment of rock. Their goal, besides earning huge revenues) was the total destruction of rock music. Since Punk was often crude, loud, indecent and vulgar, it was deprecatingly referred to as "punk rock" (having more than one meaning). Confined mostly to Europe, it never achieved universal acclaim. However, Johnny Rotten and the Sex Pistols, Blondie, Ian Drurry and the Blockheads, and others left a contribution greater being mere than names to drop at cocktail parties.

Punk fundamentally influenced *New Wave*—a more sophisticated and advanced form of punk. Besides adhering to the Punk 's conviction in shock value, The Clash, Talking Heads, and others emphasized esoteric lyrics running the gamut from meandering on the Spanish Civil War to the Mechanization of the Workforce. As goes society, so goes music.

Rap holds a much greater appeal than either Punk or New Wave. Since MTV's debut, and the concomitant influence of Michael Jackson, dance has become vital to rap. Words are spoken rhythmically, following the natural stresses of the syllables and producing a singsong type of chanting. Dancers augment visualization and add to the emphasis of the text. Frequently there is a lead rapper, a backup rapper and a rhythm rapper, thus paralleling in structure a rock group. Obviously, rap uses basically no melodic elements as the words are the driving force. Originally, rap was exclusively dominated by black groups, but since Vanilla Ice, white rappers have become respectable. Even the Annual Grammy Awards recognizes the best of the year's rappers.

An interesting phenomenon of rock is the organization of benefit concerts—addressing such issues as racism, injustice, poverty, war, and world hunger. In 1985 ten million dollars in relief was raised for Ethiopian hunger victims, with a recording *Do they know it's Christmas?* In that same year Live Aid raised forty million dollars for African hunger relief and Farm Aid began yearly benefits for the American farmer. The most memorable song of these events is unquestionably *We are the World*, which premiered at the live aid concert, viewed by an estimated one and one billion people globally.

Will rock survive into the next century? The question, though legitimate, is most relevant since rock shows no sign of slowing down. Nevertheless, rock is increasingly being enriched by other music and cultures. For instance, Latin-American beats, Jamaican cadences, and African rhythms are broadcasting this infusion. Additionally, jazz also is being tapped for its rich tradition and innovative style. Indeed, there is no telling what will be next.

Bibliography

Belz Carl, The story of rock. Oxford University Press, NY. 1972.

Prince, Dorough. *Popular Music Culture in America* Ardsley House, 1992.

Taylor, Derek. *It was Twenty Years Ago*. Simon and Schuster. 1989.

Palmer, Tony *The Rolling Stones*. Rolling Stones Press, NY , 1983.

Film and TV Composers

Many composers of the Post World War II years wrote music for the popular medium of film and television. Here is a partial list of composers and some of their work:

John Williams (1932-) Star Wars, Close Encounters, Lost in Space etc.

Lalo Schiffin (1932 -) Mission Impossible etc.

Andre Previn 0 929 -) Street Car Named Desire etc.

Leonard Bernstein (1918-1990) West Side Story

Igor Stravinsky (1882 - 1971) lived in Hollywood

Sergei Prokofiev (1891-1953)

Dimitri Shostakovich (1906- 1975) wrote music for many Russian films

John Corigliano (1938- _) wrote the film score for the "Red Violin" 1996

George Auric (1899- 78) French films with Jean Cocteau, also "Moulin Rouge"

Herbie Hancock (1940-) Jazz pianist and composer, film score for Death Wish

Jerry Goldsmith: music for "Twilight Zone" and Star Trek television series.

Some films that used music of the masters:

Mozart: Piano Concerto No. 21, Adagio—for the film "Evira Madigan" 1967

Mozart: Clarinet Concerto in A major for the film "Out of Africa"

Mozart: diverse selections for "Amadeus"

Puccini: Che Gelida Manina (from La Bohème) in "Moonstruck" 1988

Puccini: Un Bel Di (Madame Butterfly) My Geisha" and "Fatal Attraction"

Vivaldi: Concerto for Mandolin, for the film "Kramer vs. Kramer" 1979

Vivaldi: music of the Four Seasons for the film of the same name.

Wagner: Ride of the Valkyries for "Apocalypse Now" 1979

Wagner: Prelude form Lohengrin Act 3, for the "Great Dictator" 1949

Beethoven: Piano Concerto No. 5 for "The Dead Poets Society" 1989

Bach: Aria from the Goldberg Variations in' Silence of the Lambs" 1992

Bach: Violin Concerto No.3 in "Love Story" 1970

Richard Strauss: Opening fanfare (Also Sprach Zarathustra) in "2001 Space Odyssey"

Ludwig van Beethoven: Symphony No. 9: 2nd mov't in "A Clockwork Orange"

Ludwig van Beethoven: Symphony No. 5: 1st mov't in "Immortal Beloved"
Rimsky Korsakov: Flight of the Bumble Bee in "Shine"
Wolfgang Amadeus Mozart: Sonata in F major in "Love Story"
Maurice Ravel: Bolero in "10"

This page is contributed by Dr. Thomas Blobner

Opera

The man who hath no name in himself,
Nor is moved with concord of sweet sounds,
Is fit for treason, stratagems and spoils...
Let no such man be trusted.
—Shakespeare

Baroque Period

The opera saw its first life light in the Baroque period, when the Gold Rush began. A hike through the Baroque period reveals a time of great opulence, emotional excesses and dynamic vitality. So it seems almost natural that in this fertile ground the opera was born. The opera, destined to become the love child of the old and the young, the palace and the humble neighborhood, was conceived by a small group of humanists, who, in 1600, tried to recreate music according to the Greek tragedies. Of course, there was no music left from the Greeks, but they knew through Plato that music was used to express the emotions of the texts.

The time was right to use the recitative, a declamatory melody which carried the story, accompanied by simple chords, as the complicated lines of counterpoint were being more and more rejected.

The monodic style (i.e. single melodic line) was already applied in the madrigals and chansons that favored the main melody and had the other voices sing only a chordal accompaniment—which, in fact, was often taken by the harpsichord or guitar. That melodic line, moreover, followed the text emotionally as well as pictorially; words like *sad, joy, high, low, death* could easily be musically illustrated.

Also, in the theater there were many plays in the Greek tragedy style, some religious plays in front of the church, and comedies with (in Italy at least) Pantalone and Pulchinella as standard jokers and entertainers. The reformers had plenty of models to work with, and soon the opera was on its way to greatness.

Claudio Monteverdi (1567-1643)

The first great opera composer was Claudio Monteverdi. He was born in Cremona, Italy, which was the center of the violinmakers; Amati and Stradivarius. Monteverdi was a singer and violinist at the court of Vincenzo Gonzaga at Mantua and in 1613 he was appointed Maestro to San Marco in Venice. He wrote an enormous quantity of music, especially madrigals, scores of religious music, motets and masses. He also composed nineteen operas, most of them lost; we have however *Orfeo (1607) L'Arianna (1608) L'Incoronazione di Poppea (1642)* his last opera at age seventy-five. Only *Orfeo* and *L'Incoronazione* seem complete; as of *L'Arianna,* only the famous lament, "lasciatemi morire (let me die) was preserved because a thousand tears welt up from a thousand breasts" every time it was sung.

The Camerata, the music reformers, considered *Orfeo* as ideal. Monteverdi expanded the recitative into something more elaborate, and thereby created the arioso. The musical ritornellos, short instrumental interjections, assured musical unity. *Orfeo* has already all the necessary elements that are still employed in the contemporary opera: the overture, chorus, recitatives, ariosos, and arias. The latter became Italy's forte: the bel canto, the triumph of glorious singing. The only element missing at this time was the ballet, soon to be added by the French.

Although the opera was first performed for the rich and famous, the Doges in Venice, not long thereafter public performances were organized. Around 1637, in Venice alone sixteen opera houses were built and each performed five operas per year. The impresarios insisted that a smaller chorus is hired, a thinner orchestra with everything geared towards solos, without taking away the glory of the Italians. Most librettos were based upon epic subjects, royal love stories, and mythological chronicles, often with references causes furor with their references to current events.

It took France somewhat longer to have their operas. Competition from the theater was very strong. Even the most ardent opera composers resorted to the ballet, to enhance the essential difference with the theater. No wonder that Lully, that consummate ballet composer, interrupts theatrical plays with ballet, very much to the consternation of Molière, when he saw dancing in his *Le Bourgeois Gentilhomme.*

Although Hamburg saved the opera in Germany, still most of the productions were imports, proving that by now that the opera had some international appeal.

Interestingly enough Bach never was involved directly with opera writing, although his cantatas and Passions, had the same format. In contrast to Handel, his compatriot, born in the same year as he wrote 39 Italian operas for London's stages—seven operas in English.

In England, the grand master of the opera is arguable Henry Purcell (1659-1695). Under the critical eyes of the Puritans the opera was not sanctioned until about 1656, just in time for Purcell to try his hand at it. Although his pitiful short life gave him only enough time for one single work in that genre. *Dido and Aeneas,* let in freely the influence of Monteverdi. It is nevertheless a masterpiece of first order. Fresh and spontaneous, even though it was commissioned for a girl's boarding school. It is amazing how closely Dido's lament is to Monteverdi's "lasciatemi morire" of *L'Arianna,* without losing its own identity. When Purcell died, England was ready for another grand slam, this time coming from a foreigner, George Frederic Handel.

Unlike Bach, he does not come from a musical family; his father was a surgeon at the court of Weissenfels. Around 1706 Handel was in Rome and soon his mission, conquering the world with his operas. In 1710 he landed in London with *Rinaldo* under his arm, written in a mere fortnight. Although the new King of England, King George I, had been his former employer at Hannover, and Handel had deserted him, the two compatriots were soon reconciled. The celebrity-driven Handel had nevertheless some bitter disappointments, in part due to changing taste of the English and some nasty rivals like Johann Adolf Hasse. Handel eventually switched to the oratorio, basically an opera with sacred text and no acting. In that genre he wrote several master works: *Judas Maccabeus, Saul, Esther and the Messiah.*

Handle's genius was very much in tune with the extravagance of the opera; even his instrumental works ooze with vocal spirit. Nevertheless, his ebullient and sumptuous bel-canto virtuosity, as described by the Italians, was not as welcome in cold rainy London. The famous *Beggar's Opera* was more popular; its paupers and pariahs were making fun of the pompous heroes of Handel's mythological world. Nowadays Handel's forty-six operas are only known by name. Was it guilt that made the English government decide to place Handel's sepulcher among the nobility in Westminster Abbey?

Rococo Period

Besides the *opera seria,* a serious subject opera, of Alessandro Scarlatti, there is a new genre brewing in sunny Naples; the *opera buffo.* The comical opera, full of drolleries and humorous situations, is less interested in the pure vocalizations of the prima donna, but rather the music become more subordinated to the play itself The pioneer of that type of opera was Giovanni Battista Pergolesi

(1710-1736). He wrote in his short life some eight operas, although the best known is, *La Serva Padrona* (the servant-mistress)—written in a minimalist style. Only three characters (and one is mute!) no chorus, and only four arias and two duets; that's it. And yet, Pergolesi set the standard, and model for all time.)When it was premiered in 1733 at the Teatro the S. Bartolomeo in Naples, *La Serva Padrona* was a sell-out and the beginning of a life of triumph. In 1752, long after Pergolesi's untimely death at twenty-six, it was introduced in Paris where Jean Jacques Rousseau, the philosopher, wrote a opera buffa, *Le Devin du Village*, in the same style, that stayed a favorite for many years in France.

Classical Period

The classical composer in the widest sense of the word is an artist, who having found the ideal form finds a perfect balance between mind and emotion, lifting both through his strong personality to a higher human level. For the Classical composers music is no longer a titillation of the ears, but a source of deep emotional expression. Beethoven puts it at a higher level than philosophy, ethics and religion, all put together. Feelings are everything, said Goethe, even though he couldn't find the correct world for it all. The audience of the Classical composers is no longer the rich and famous, but the common man and the amateur with genuine appreciation for the beauty of the human expression.

If the literary center was Weimar, with Goethe and Schiller, for music it was Vienna. The Austrian capital was, as Mozart writes in 1781 to his father: "... a marvelous place and the best city in the world for my craft." The Classical composers at that time Gluck, Haydn, Mozart, or Beethoven, all were writing operas galore. Obviously, there was an eager audience waiting for their newest productions.

Christoph-Willibald Gluck (1714- 1787) was born in a lost corner of Bavaria. As soon as he was old enough he was on the road: first to Italy to learn his craft, then London, and finally Vienna. He also made many side trips to Paris, virtually his second home. Opera was his calling and he managed to write 107 of them, although none in German! Gluck is really a transitional figure, but a reformer nonetheless. He eliminated the squeaky harpsichord, the recitatives and the excesses of the prima donna's ornamentation of the arias. The chorus is reintroduced and part of the action, and the ballet is no longer a necessary evil, but integrated into the fabric of the drama. The overture reflects the themes and sets the tone of the opera. His reforms caused a storm of protest, and there was a substantial bout between Gluckists and Puccinists; in the end Gluck's revisions stuck! His best and most successful opera is arguably *Orfeo*, followed by *Alceste*.

Haydn's (1733-1809) reputation was built mainly on his 83 string quartets and his 104 symphonies. Nevertheless Haydn wrote some eighteen operas, five children's operas and at least six arias for theater plays. Most of the operas were intended for the magnificent theater at Esterház.

Mozart (1756-1791) was born in the Rococo fantasyland of Salzburg. Together with his equally precocious sister he toured most of Europe as a Wunderkind. After many exhausting trips through Germany, France, Belgium, England, Holland and Italy, he finally settled in the magical city of Vienna. Not for long, as he died at barely thirty-five. His remains were buried in a mass grave: a shrill dissonance upon the life that seemed so blessed by the smiling gods. But his music lives on.

Melody is the greatest secret of Mozart's genius. His melodies are generous and very singable while never running out of fresh invention. This was nowhere more appreciated than in his operas. That together with his fine intuition, intelligent and objective human observation and the glow of his warm personality made him an opera composer per excellence. Nowhere else are female characters better portrayed than by Mozart. Unforgettable is the tender melancholy of the countess in *Figaro*, the sensuality of Elvira and the proud sincerity of Donna Anna in *Don Giovanni*. Also the many contrasting couples: Constance and Belmonte in the *Abduction from the Seraglio*, and the simple people like Blöndchen and Pedrill, or the aristocratic Tamino and Pamina in contrast to Papageno and Papagena in the *Magic Flute*. Mozart has a knack of mixing comical situations with tragic events, playing masterfully the strings of humor and irony: the cynical laugh of Leporello in *Don Giovanni*, the empathetic smile of Figaro in the *Marriage of Figaro*. It become an impossible task to try to select Mozart's greatest opera. Is it his buffa-like *Marriage of Figaro* of 1786 or *Così fan tutte*—or is it his opera seria *Idomeneo* of 1781 versus *La Clemenza di Tito* of 1791—or shall we select his German Singspiel *The Magic Flute*? Maybe Mozart said it best himself when he wrote his father about his propensity to opera: "having them talk about opera, and hearing them sing in the opera house makes me exceedingly happy" (1777).

Ludwig van Beethoven (1770-1827) was born of an abusive alcoholic father. In 1787 he went to Vienna and impressed Mozart, who must have said: "Pay attention! He will have the world talk about him!" In 1792 he made Vienna his permanent address. By 1796 he experienced his first painful sensations of deafness, and by 1800 his hearing was completely lost. This tragedy brings him to deepest despair. Beethoven withdrew more and more from society and found solace in his music.

In 1803 Beethoven wrote his first and only opera. Schikaneder, who had commissioned Mozart's *Magic Flute,* had asked Beethoven to compose an opera for his newly acquired Theater-an-der-Wien. The suggested popular play of Bouilly, *Lénore, ou L'amour Conjugal* (Leonore, or the Marital love), was selected by the new director, Baron von Braun. It proved to be a contrived and antiquated libretto, fascinating Beethoven himself but never a crowd-pleaser. The premiere was a disaster. Napoleon's troops were occupying Vienna and the audience was mostly soldiers, coming only to kill time. Also the work proved to be too long, too boring and too dull. In 1806 a revised version was performed, and received somewhat better. Unluckily Beethoven got into a bitter dispute about the box-office revenues. Again the work was withdrawn. At long last in 1814, after a complete overhaul and completely rewritten overture, his time entitled *Fidelio,* the opera finally found some success. Even today the opera is seldom performed.

Beethoven, exhausted from all the intrigues and badly stung by the many disappointments, never again wrote another opera.

Romantic Period

The Classical era's opera masterworks undoubtedly culminated with Mozart. Eminent successors of the next rank included: Weber, Rossini, Berlioz, Donizetti, Verdi, Wagner, Gounod, and Bizet. Besides these, the Russian National School began with Glinka's *Life for the Tsar* (1836), Mussorgsky's *Boris Godunov* (performed in 1894), along with Rimsky-Korsakov and Tchaikovsky.

Opera seems almost designed for the Romantic era. If indeed the Romantic artists revolt against eighteenth century rationalism and rather exalt in individual emotion and the world of fantasy, illusion, and the grotesque. The life of the artist became increasingly unconventional, shunning the restraints and intolerance of the petit bourgeois. Artists suffered, knowing that their dreams and reality could not be bridged under the ruling leadership. This duality is discernible in most artists of the Romantic era. All of the arts reflected these divergent expressions:

light and darkness

reverence and disrespect

truth and deceit

intimacy and exuberance

sadness and laughter

asceticism and eroticism

Dichotomies were expressed within the same work. These dualities make Romanticism the land of   contrasts. Increasingly, literature—especially works by Goethe and Shakespeare—inspired music. Archtypical dualities and great literature combined to create the recipe for great operas.

Romantic opera's first great master is Carl Maria von Weber (1786-1826.) Although von Weber wrote certain noteworthy orchestral compositions, it is as creator of the Romantic German opera that he became immortal. Romantic opera's first salvo was struck in *Freischutz* (the Free Shooter) (1821.) Here we first hear hunters singing amid fragrant woods. We also hear the evening bells, where hunters love simple maidens and where the devil himself raises havoc. In *Euryanthe* (1823), the audience is presented a medieval play. In *Oberon* we hear the horns of romance and dreams, giving us a magical excursion into the kingdom of fairies, elves, and Eastern wonders. Within a month after its triumphant London premiere, Weber died of consumption. Even in his brief life, Weber paved the way to the music dramas of Wagner (1813-1883.)

Wagner's work crowns the apex of German Romantic opera. Born in the Bach city of Leipzig Wagner studied theater and literature, under the influence of his step-father. His life combined triumphs and failure. He first triumphed, as opera conductor in Magdeburg, Koninsbergen, and, Riga; he then shamefully fled his debtors, to Paris. Following Meyerbeer's intervention, he acquired a new position in Dresden, where he wrote his first masterpiece *Rienzi*. Afterwards, his involvement in the revolution forced moves again to Paris and ultimately to Switzerland. There he wrote anti-Semitic pamphlets, directed against Meyerbeer and Mendelssohn. In Zurich, Wagner composed his greatest work, *Tristan und Isolde*, while romancing Mathilda Wesendonck, wife of his supporter! The 1959 General Amnesty allowed his return to Germany where Ludwig II became his generous patron. Intrigues of jealous courtiers destroyed that financially rewarding relationship. Meantime, Wagner lived with Cosima Liszt, his second wife to be, after his first wife's death. After his Bavarian adventure, Wagner returned to

Switzerland, briefly becoming Nietzsche's idol. In 1872 Wagner built the Festspielhaus in Bayreuth, the dream of his ambitions. This became his operatic temple and pilgrims' shrine.

His influence can hardly be exaggerated as he—especially after writing *Tristan,*—was obsessed with the *Gesamtkunst,* integrating all of the operatic arts. The subjects were mostly either ancient Germanic sagas or other myths of the Middle Ages. The music was an integral part of the drama and not merely a display of bravura arias and other isolated pieces. The aim of the "music drama" was no longer to entertain, but as Nietzsche said, "The music is a world philosophy, the drama only its mirror, the shadow of this idea." The orchestra is no mere musical accompaniment, but the unfolding drama's backbone, interpreting every emotion and participating fully in the drama at hand. Melodies are created in endless sequences' harmonies are full of dissonant chromatic alterations undermining our sense of tonality. Repeatedly the tonic is avoided, strongly conveying unrest and urgency. Those many dissonances in the inner voices give the music a strong sense of independence. The master of Bayreuth dominated his era's music. Scores of composers became devout Wagnerians.

The exact antipode to Wagner was Verdi. Born in 1813 near Parma, he always remained proud of his farm background. As a newlywed, his young wife and two children soon died. Verdi almost relinquished his "opera career," but in 1842 his *Nabudccodonosor* made him famous overnight. He was the icon of the freedom fighters—his very name sounding like the anagram for independence: **VERDI** = Vittore Emmanuele, **Re** (king) **D'**Italia. Between 1851 and 1887 he wrote numerous masterpieces; *Rigoletto, il Trovatore, La Traviata, Aida,* and in 1887 his greatest opera a *Requiem* honoring his friend, the poet Manzoni. While in his eighties, Verdi wrote two more master works: *Othello* and *Falstaff,* both based on Shakespeare plays.

Unlike Wagner, Giuseppe Verdi wrote for the people. His melodies, very singable and imminently Italian, assured his great popularity. The orchestra is at best completely at the singers' disposition. He retains the old form of numbers-opera, nothing refined, no bel-canto, but with a folksy direct intent at times broaching vulgarity. He remained popular, even now. Although Verdi understood Wagner's reforms, Verdi sometimes imitated, nevertheless he stayed miles from his German counterpart. If Wagner created sophisticated music, Verdi always had the marketplace in mind. Nietzsche, was became disenchanted with the pathos of Wagner, called to "Mediterraneanize the music," he must have unquestionably having Verdi in mind. Opera with an inevitable fatality, nature, health, optimism, youth, and sound morality is what the German philosopher must have discovered in the southern fervor of the Italian master.

Some other composers will follow in the footsteps of Verdi: Pietro Mascagni, Leoncavallo, and, of course, the ever popular Puccini.

One of the first French composers to fall under the influence of realism, an imitation of the novelists, was George Bizet (1838-1875). This was especially evident in his most famous work, *Carmen*. The very choice of the subject, the love and hate in the Spanish factories and smugglers, dens, reflects a realistic milieu-painting of everyday life. His use of flamenco dances and Iberian songs, the refined orchestration of the score, the sharp character differentiation of the personages and its fatalistic outcome made *Carmen* one of the most performed operas ever.

Meanwhile in Russia, the music began to stir. Mussorgsky was the most gifted of the so-called "Mighty Five," a group of young dilettantes proclaiming, in a shrill manifesto, their independence of the German music. Mussorgsky was at 20, in his salad days, still a daring young salon officer, but he soon resigned to become a composer. With poverty, loneliness, and distain he paid his genius: he chose to live with the farm workers so as not to pollute his inspiration with the noises and criticisms of the big city. He died at 42, an alcoholic, homeless derelict. His master work is the opera *Boris Godunov* (1874). Often his melodies are rooted in the Russian folk music and the Russian speech pattern. Although he uses some very sharp dissonances, those harsh chords are always there to heighten the dramatic tensions and intense emotions, Mussorgsky had little musical schooling and yet with limited means he evokes powerful, intense, dramatic scenes. He was a prophet.

Impressionistic Period

Debussy, who's cradle stood in Paris, called himself "Musicien Français"—French musician—very much implying that he wanted to be the antidote to both Verdi and especially to the overpowering fascination with Wagner's chromatic infusion. His *Prelude à l'apres-midi d'un faune* was also the prelude to a new century, a new era, and a new music. *Toute ma musique s'efforce a n'être que melodie, so* countered Debussy to his critics. But his melodies are surprisingly new; sometimes with a capriciousness of nimble arabesques, sometimes with simple lines, absorbing all the nuances necessary for flexible declarations. Seldom will his melody become overly pathetic, but it usually stays on the side of the tender emotion. His harmonies are bathed in subtle dissonances, the poetic richness of the nine chords and the minor dominant seven chords. While Debussy's dissonance never hurts, he also favors the parallel running chords, more a color scheme than just clever ways of harmonizing:

Debussy's sole opera can be summarized in one word: *raffiné* (refined). And very French, like those exquisite pastries and artful entremets, of which only the Cordon Bleu chefs know the secret recipes. The orchestra finally yields its dominant role and no word or melody is smothered by heavy chords or blaring brass. In spite of the intricate drama we are transported into a dream world. The old label, "it is Impressionistic," will no longer serve with its easy characterization.

Twentieth Century

After Wagner and Debussy's experiments, circa 1910, music was at the rim of the abyss; dissonance was gaining increasingly more ground; rhythm shed its strong ordered straight jacket; melody negated its former pleasing qualities; and form broke through all the limitations of its blueprint edicts. Most composers born between 1875 and 1890 took the most daring consequences. Most radical was the 12-tone school under the guidance of Schoenberg. Stravinsky radicalizes the rhythm, the soul of his Russian expressionism and Bartok will, with the help of folk music, find new sounds, new rhythms, and new melodies. As of 1922-1925, they all formulated a neo-classicism, milder in tone, but based on their new technical discoveries.

Toward the 1960s, yet another new trend seems to emerge, and while most of the leading composers are still at work, it would be preposterous to try to formulate their living creed.

Alban Berg (1885-1935) is Schoenberg's most gifted disciple. He wrote two operas in his short life, Wozzeck (1922) being his best-known work, written to the text of George Büchner (1813-1837), a German dramatist and forerunner of Expressionism. It is the sordid story of a common soldier pressured into murdering his unfaithful mistress. He too perishes in a nearby swamp trying to find the murder weapon. At the end of the drama, his little girl plays undisturbed with some neighbor children, near her father's body. Chilling, especially since the language is sometimes quite vulgar and vile, with some strong tendencies toward madness and hallucinations. With Wozzeck, Berg proved that the cerebral 12-tone music, with some liberal deviations, could express strong feelings, and the atonal harmonies could be tolerated without being inevitably offensive to the average opera goer's ears. His music rises from the depths of his soul, reaching the deepest emotions, and the gore and heart-rending anguish of post-war Vienna.

Bela Bartok wrote only one opera, *Bluebeard's Castle,* in 1911, based on the well-known fairy tale of Charles Perrault. In that story, Bluebeard's new wife is given the household keys that will open all the doors except one. She opens the forbidden door and finds hanging severed heads of his former wives. Only when Bluebeard is slain by her brothers is she rescued. It is a highly symbolic work, rich in meaning but at times unclear and obscure in its intentions, going from bestial cruelty and lust for power to the pleasures of gold and jewels and the peaceable kingdom of Bluebeard. Bartok found the right musical expression for each part. Although it was deemed "unperformable" by the deciding Philistines of the Commission of Fine Arts, the possible producers of the work-, twenty years later it resurfaced.

Igor Stravinsky (1882-1971) wrote several operas: *The Nightingale* after Hans Christian Anderson, *Maura* after Pushkin, *The Rakes Progress* on W. H. Auden after Hogarth, and *Oedipus Rex* on a Jean Cocteau text (1927) after Sophocles.

The latter work, *Oedipus Rex,* an opera-oratorio, was written in Latin. As Stravinsky said, Latin was indirectly suggested to him by St. Francis of Assisi, who used to speak French when he wanted to express some profoundity. It was to become one of Stravinsky's major works; it also was the consecration of a new austerity, monumental, with a classic dignity. He expressly required that the staging should be limited to exits and entrances, as Oedipus, Jocasta, and Creon rigidly stand as living statues. Although billed as opera, it comes across as an oratorio, and yet, the staging of the tableaux gives welcome relief to the music— while the music keeps its dominant role. Despite its outward stiffness, the music carries some exquisite passages, some angry music for Oedipus, but also some tender passages when Oedipus finds out who he is. The use of the chorus is most effective, as were Bach's, in his Passions and Handel's in his Messiah. This is a worthy interpretation of Sophocles' drama.

United States

Interestingly, the opera in the United States, along with jazz, contributed enormously to the twentieth century culture. In the process, the name opera was dropped and substituted with "musical," or "musical comedy," and even sometimes the words "Broadway revue" have been used. Most musicals, in contrast to opera, are lighter fare, with simpler tunes and harmony, using a smaller pitch range than the grand opera arias. Very often, the musicals are the work of a collective effort; the "book" and the song lyrics, the tunes, the orchestration, the overture, and interludes are often divided among several collaborators. The musical sprouted from *vaudeville*—a variety show with songs, dances, juggling, acrobats, etc., but usually no plot as such. From the turn of the century until the 1920's, the United States boasted about 10,000 vaudeville theaters.

After the "rock music revolution" of the 1960s, only a few of the musicals were affected. Rock elements were heard in *Jesus Christ Superstar* (1971), *Evita* (1979), *Cats* (1982), and, *The Phantom of the Opera* (1987), all by the English composer Andrew Lloyd Webber. Stephen Sondheim seems to ride at the edge of musical and opera, especially in his *Sweeney Todd, the Demon Barber of Fleet Street* (1984).

George Gershwin (1898-1937) always wanted to write an American *Carmen* with the beauty of Wagner's *Meistersinger, as* he himself always said. In 1935 he settled on *Porgy and Bess,* after DuBose Heyward's story, with lyrics by Ira Gershwin. Bess is the flirtatious Eve, Crown her hard-drinking husband Sporting Life a snake and dope vendor, and finally Porgy, who finds a new youth because of his relation with Bess. It is a tragic story.

Gershwin made many trips to Charleston, S.C., to listen to the black people, their songs and spirituals, and visited their churches, homes, and nightclubs in his search for musical inspiration. Gershwin worked twenty months on the opera, and when completed in September, 1935, it was performed 124 times. But, it wound up losing its complete investment and was considered a box office failure. The critical acclaim also was mixed! Now it has become America's greatest homegrown opera.

In 1957, a landmark musical, West Side Story, was written by Leonard Bernstein, a leading conductor, concert pianist, and composer of serious orchestral works and television lecturer for the Young People's Concerts with the New York Philharmonic. It was not his first musical, but was by far his most popular, especially since it was developed into an Oscar-winning film (1961). The story is a modem day version of Shakespeare's *Romeo and Juliet,* set in New York's West Side slums, and deals with gang rivalry and youthful love.

The "American musical" also had some followers abroad and no one succeeded better than Andrew Lloyd Webber, who has captivated audiences worldwide. At age twenty-three, he wrote his first "Rock-opera," *Jesus Christ Superstar*, followed rapidly by *Evita, Cats,* and *The Phantom of the Opera*. The latter musical is based on Gaston Leroux's novel, a larger-than-life romantic story of a disfigured phantom, who lives beneath the Paris Opera House. He falls for Christine, whom he relentlessly pursues. He teaches her singing and through intrigue and murder, makes her a star. But, he makes her choose between Raoul, her lover, and himself. Eventually, she saves Raoul's life by kissing the Phantom, who is so moved that he grants them both freedom, while he disappears forever. The great success of Webber's musicals is simply their appeal to the audience, who identify with both the music and the story.

> *Who the artist is, and where he lives, is to the*
> *average person more important than what he created.*
> —Goethe

Opera Chronological List

Baroque 1600-1750

Peri, *Euridice* 1600

Monteverdi, wrote 19 operas. *Orfeo 1607, Popea 1642*

Lully and Rameau wrote several operas each.

Vivaldi wrote perhaps as many as 39 operas, most them lost

Purcell, wrote 5 operas, *Dido and Aeneas 1689*

Pergolesi, *La serva padrone* 1733

Handel wrote 46 operas, all Italian type

Bach, Johann Christian, wrote 13 operas.

Classical 1750-1830

Gluck wrote some 50 operas: *Orpheus*

Mozart 22 operas: *Bastien and Bastienne 1768* Mozart was 12! *The Marriage of Figaro 1786, Don Giovanni 1787, The Magic Flute 1791*

Rossini wrote 40 operas: *The Barber of Seville 1816, William Tell 1829*

Beethoven, one opera *Fidelio 1805*

Romantic 1830-1910

Schubert wrote 15 operas, *Rosamunde 1823*

Weber, Wrote 7 operas, *Der Freischatz 1821*

Donizetti 75 operas: *Lucia di Lammermoor 1835*

Glinka wrote two operas *Russlan and Ludmilla 1834*

Mendelssohn wrote seven operas *Midsummer Night's dream 1842*

Berlioz wrote 3 operas *Benvenuo Cellini 1834*

Smetana wrote 9 operas *The Bartered Bride 1863*

Verdi wrote 32 operas *Rigoletto 1851 Falstaff 1893*

Wagner wrote 15 operas *Tristan and Isolde 1857, Parsifal 1877*

Tchaikovsky wrote 11 operas *Eugene onegin 1877*

Mussorgsky wrote 12 operas, most unfinished except *Boris Godunov 1874*

Bizet wrote 24 operas *Carmen 1875*

Saint-Saëns wrote 13 operas. *Samson and Delilah 1877*

Massenet wrote 27 operas, *Manon 1884*

Mascagni many operas, mostly failures except *Cavalleria Rusticana 1890*

Borodin wrote one unfinished opera *Prince Igor 1890*

Puccini wrote 11 operas *La Bohème 1893 Madame Butterfly 1904*

Twentieth Century

Debussy wrote one opera *Pellías et Mélisande 1902*

Ravel wrote 2 operas *L'Enfant et les Sortilèges 1917-25*

Janácek wrote 10 operas *Jenufa 1904*

De Falla wrote 2 operas *La vida breve 1913*

Bartók wrote 3 operas *The Miraculous Manderin 1919*

Stravinsky wrote 5 operas *The Rake's Progress 1951*

Honegger wrote 5 operas *Jeanne D'Arc 1938*

Schoenberg wrote 2 operas *Moses and Aaron 1932*

Berg wrote 2 operas *Wozzeck 1921*

Hindemith wrote 7 operas *Mathis der Mahler 1938*

Weill wrote 15 operas *Dreigroschenoper 1928*

Gershwin wrote one opera *Porgy and Bess 1935*

Shostakovitch 3 operas *Lady Macbeth 1934*

Orff wrote 8 operas *Carmina Burana 1936*

Britten wrote 7 operas *Peter Grimes 1945*

Menotti wrote 8 operas *Amahl and the Night Visitors 1951*

Bernstein wrote 2 operas (musicals) *West Side story 1957*

Schönberg, Claude-Michel wrote 2 musicals *Les Misérables 1986, Miss Saigon 1990*

Andrew Lloyd Webber wrote at least 9 musicals *Cats 1980, Jesus Christ Superstar 1985, The Phantom of the Opera 1987, Evita 1990*

Music of Other Cultures

Let us not forget that delight must be
the basis and aim of all musical art.
—Rossini

Some Generalizations on Nonwestern Music

Some five thousand years ago, the first urban civilizations began in three specific areas, Mesopotania (today's Iran), Egypt, and Crete. Writing likely began first among Mesopotania's Sumerians. Their highly organized society instituted an alphabet; architecture's arch, columns, and vaults; the calendar; and a government ruled by laws—long predating Egyptian culture. Subsequently, the Egyptians, Cretans, Hittites, Phoenicians, Syrians, and Hebrews each developed distinctly featured cultures. One such unique feature was music. Most probably, each culture's music had its own unique characteristics. Unfortunately, neither the Sumerians, Egyptians, nor Cretans wrote music that we can decipher or read. While scholars maintain that some written music exists among the hieroglyphs, there is no way of even remotely guessing how it sounded. This becomes even more tantalizing since their large collection of paintings, sculptures, and poems all allude to music ... music with ever elusive notations. Although musical notations remain baffling, must the music itself also remain *forever* elusive?

Have we foolishly discounted the oral tradition? Is that ancient music discernible in today's Arabian music? Noting that musical instruments have remained markedly similar, that both scales and modes still distinguish that music, and that its many strange sounding rhythms remain, apparently the answer is unequivocally—yes. Viewing Egyptian paintings of lovely girls playing their flute and lute for the Pharaoh, or examining prints of ladies dancing for some festive event to a blind harpist's tunes, it seems entirely possible it may be similar to Arabian contemporary music. Ancient chants may reverberate in later Gregorian music, as perpetuated in our own Christian liturgy. Since Sumeria, Babylon, Assyria, and Egypt were theocratic states, music was stressed in their worship. What survived of this great tradition? Possibly some music found its way into contemporary Arabian music. Instruments had been equated with divine beings, cosmic forces, and other essentials of daily living. Thus, if Arabian religions survived, why would not their music?

The Old Testament, mentions numerous instruments, including:

drums

lyres with strings made of sheep intestines

harps

zithers with 10 strings

flutes

lutes

mizmaar (a sort of oboe)

horns

shofar or ram's horn

trumpets

a jingling instrument similar to our triangle, cymbals.

During the Crusades, many of those instruments were brought back from Eastern countries, particularly Egypt. Musicians enlivened festivals, soothed the gods, gladdened men, drove evil from birthing mothers; even the ancient Song of the Harper urges: "Call no halt to music and dance, but bid all care be gone."

Undoubtedly, songs traversed the Psalms, the rather candidly erotic *Song of Songs*, and the marriage liturgy. But how? Unfortunately their written notation remain our enigma.

Arabian Music

The rhythm of Arabian music (closely related to Hindu music) is extremely interesting. The rhythmic arrangement is usually 2 + 3 + 3 beats, all supported by a hand drum, the *tabla*. Major instruments include: lutes, the short-necked ud, and the long-necked tambur. There is also the double shawm and two pipes, one for the melody, the other for the bourdon accompaniment. Despite Islamic's secular music having vast variances, their religious music was extremely limited—only the call to prayer's chanting and the sacred Koran was tolerated. Despite Mohammed's contradictory pronouncements regarding music, the Arabs evidenced great musical passion. Poetry remains strongly linked to music. As one example, *A Thousand and One Nights* was essentially sung. Minstrels were engaged at the courts, and most were highly skilled in poetry—singing, instrument playing, and composing. Moreover, the wealthy often employed harems of singers and dancers. Music encompassed religious life, and to a larger extent, secular society.

The musical scales contain 17 tones, with many notes a quarter-tone below the whole-tone steps, for example below C, D, E, G, A. Some curious combinations resulted. The Arab influence upon Spanish music is rightly noted. The Moors having been in Spain for some 700 years were bound to leave a mark. True, European music owes their instruments (lutes, drums), especially in some of the guitar music, but most other sweeping claims crumble under closer scrutiny. Nevertheless, is flamenco music free of the Arabian tradition, even though it has Sephardic Jewish and Byzantine traditions in them?

Flamenco dancing, with its erotic body movements, finger snapping, feet stomping and hand clapping, is decidedly from Andulusia and associated with the Gypsies of southern Spain. It is there that the Moors stayed the longest and only left Granada in 1491. Did they leave some traces in the flamenco dances?

African Music

One cannot ignore tropical Africa's music. Although it has no written tradition, like the music of other continents, it has a rich and varied heritage of sayings, stories, legends, and sagas. All were transmitted to us in the form of songs. Some tribes have hundreds of songs, created for every imaginable occasion, including: weddings, births, initiations, prayers for rain, fertility, installation of chiefs, healing, death, and burials. Musicians achieved a surprising variety of sounds from the materials they had, particularly from the many shapes of drums and other percussion instruments. They even had a "talking" drum, an hourglass shaped drum carried on the player's shoulder, so versatile that they could tell stories and send messages to other far away villages. Besides their drums, they had a whole arsenal of bells, rattles, scrapers, xylophones (sometimes with twenty slats) and log drums (sometimes tree trunks over twenty feet long—all to be used later in jazz and the South American music.)

The slaves did not come empty handed, but in fact brought their culture with them, especially in the form of songs, dances, and their diversified rhythms. These same rhythms fertilizing the jazz culture in the United States and in South America, is so pervasive that it forever changed the music of the Americas. That gift is not only present in a forest clearing in Uganda or Ghana, but in dance halls of their adopted country. Their vocal music also left a lasting impression, for instance, the chorus music, as it is the art of using a wide variety of vocal sounds. Singers shift from a relaxed tone to some shrill and tight sounds, occasionally imitating animal noises through grunting, whispering, shouting, and even yodeling. The singers frequently sing over ostinatos played by a myriad of percussion instruments producing a complex polyrhythmic texture. As in jazz, most of their music consists of short phrases, repeated incessantly with different words.

Music of India

Rather than speaking of music from India, we really should be talking about Hindu music. The music in India is essentially a spiritual exercise, a spiritual happening. As Ravi Shankar (born 1920) writes, "The highest aim of our music is to reveal the essence of the universe it reflects; ... through music, one can reach God." Most Indian musicians study with a guru (master-teacher) and the music tradition is passed orally, from master to disciple, who learns by imitating, as many of the musical phrases and elaborations are not, and cannot be notated (like our own blues, or the fiddle music of the Appalachian region.)

Improvisation is vital in Indian music. Their improvisations arise from a complicated system of melodic patterns (raga) and an equally complex and sophisticated system of rhythm (tala) Melodies often proceed by microtones and microtonal ornaments—and since most of their music is based on the human voice, the music navigates in approximately four octaves. Unlike Western music, Indian music is in unison, over a drone bass by a *tambura,* a long-necked lute with four strings, and a drummer, who maintains the rhythmic beat and structure.

The most popular instrument is the *sitar,* used especially in northern India and the *vina* favored in the south of India. The sitar is the more complicated instrument, with its seven strings: five for melodies, and the other two for drone effects. Besides those strings, the instrument has some nine to thirteen sympathetic vibrating strings, giving it its characteristic identity. The *tambura* is a four-strings, giving it its characteristic identity. The tambura is a four-stringed long-necked lute, used mostly as a drone in the background. The *sarod* is similar, but plucked with a coconut shell, having six strings, four for the melody and two for the drone and rhythmic background. The most important drum is the *tabla,* a pair of single-headed drums, played with the right and left hand respectively playing the tonic and the bass. Manipulated by their full hand or fingers, can produce a great variety of pitches and tone colors. Since the Indian people are so naturally gifted in poetry their music also is very much vocal. Temples maintained troupes of choristers and dancers, "servants of the gods," as they were called. They enhanced the sacred services with ritual dances, music, and hymns.

Interestingly, Indian music significantly influenced The Beatles, especially via the sitarist, Ravi Shankar. Also, the music of the French Olivier Messiaen and his disciples are heavily indebted to the music of India, particularly the rhythmic aspect. Messiaen's *Turangalila-Symphonie*, a Sanskrit word for love song, is very much beholden to the theories of melody and rhythm as practiced in the Hindu music.

Chinese Music

Although China's music spans 4000 years, yet it is the music of which we know the least. As in all previous great civilizations, music occupies a central position in its society. The tones on which the Chinese music is based have been calculated to strict mathematical principles by astronomers, as they saw there a connection between earth and heaven.

Today the Chinese ethnic music only lives on in folksongs and as ceremonial music for traditional weddings, funerals, and the like.

Most of the melodies fit within a pentatonic scale, which are transposed according to the month and the hour of the day. All their melodies belong to one of the possible five modes, each with a different fundamental tone. The rhythmic patterns were less involved than the music of India.

Ancient Chinese instruments are usually categorized according to the material they are made of:

Metal
All types of bells, gongs, and bronze drums.

Stone
Sonorous stone, mostly jade, are bells similar to the above.

Clay
Small pipes, like ocarinas, the size of goose eggs, and mostly lacquered.

Skin
Drums. Drummers were very important and looked upon as leaders.

Bamboo
Flutes, panpipes, and some sort of mouth organ (pipes set in gourds.)

Silk
Zither: k'in, with five silk strings and its variant she, which has about 50 strings. The k'in is about eight inches wide and four feet long, the she is somewhat larger. Even today the k'in players are held in high esteem. In Japan, these will be called *koto*.

Music of Japan

In an indirect way the Japanese music owes a great debt both spiritually and culturally to China. They adopted not only their religion, although adapted into Zen, but also the arts of medicine, architecture and music. They took over the Chinese pentatonic scales and most of their instruments. In fact, most of the Chinese music lives stronger in the imperial court in Japan, while it has largely disappeared in China, by name the *gagaku* (literally "graceful music".) Claude Debussy heard the gagaku at the World Exhibition in Paris in 1889 and used it in his *Poissons d'or* for piano.

Most Japanese instruments had been imported from China. The Japanese *Koto* is a variety of the Chinese Vin. The Japanese *hichiriki*, an oboe, had its equivalent in China. The Japanese *shakuhachi*, a long flute, and the *shamisen*, are both characteristic of Japan. The *shamisen*, also of Chinese origin, is a favorite of the geishas, who are renowned for their skill in music, poetry, dancing, as well as the art of love. Court musicians were exempted from taxes and the profession, even today, is strictly hereditary. In Japan, as in China, music is closely related to poetry and mime, and performers often accompany themselves on the koto, shamisen, or the flute.

The most characteristic instrument is arguably the koto, a narrow but long instrument (about four feet) with thirteen strings—originally of silk now mostly nylon. Like Buddhism and wood block printing, the koto also was imported from China. About 650 A.D. Chinese and Korean musicians came to play for the Japanese emperor in his court orchestra. There, they formed the famous *gagaku* orchestra, as mentioned before, and they brought along their own instruments, among them an instrument that later on would be called the koto. The great masterpieces of the koto were from 1615 to roughly 1868, when Japan isolated itself from the outside world and other cultures. During this incubation period, Japan reinvented itself and the wood blocks became more colorful and the kabuki theater, a form of drama was outfitted with brilliant music and stylistic dances. The koto was no longer the domain of religious music by priests and scholars, but was emancipated to be used as entertainment by musicians belonging to special guilds. Many musicians were blind, and because of their handicap, most traditional music was passed down from teacher to student by rote. Only since World War II is there a system of notation in place. The most famous teacher, composer, and performer of music for the koto is Yatsuhashi Kengyo (1614-1685), considered today as founder of modern koto music.

Most of the music of the koto is pentatonic (5=tone scale) with notes that correspond to A, B, C, E, F on our piano. But besides the limited scale, great emphasis is placed in the way the sounds are produced: tone color, dynamic level, pitch variation, and ornamentations are of highest importance. Among the latter are harmonics, similar to those of a violin, glissando, vibrato, pulling of the strings either away or towards the player, tapping of the instrument, not unlike the Spanish flamenco guitar. Playing the koto is a highly refined art.

Music of Bali

Bali is one of the 3,000 Indonesian islands. As in many Oriental countries, the arts and music were heavily indebted to the Chinese, Hindu, and Islamic cultures. The islands were colonized from India in early times and their religion is still very much Hindu. Until the arrival of the Dutch (1595-1949) no one knew of them. As in India, the music and dances are very much associated with worship, and ritually offered as sacrifice to the gods. But what makes their music so special is the *gamelan*, a highly developed orchestra, which plays at various provincial court functions and in the villages for their festivities and dances. The orchestra has a wide variety of percussion instruments made out of wood, bronze, bamboo, and clay. The "melody" instruments are mainly a two-stringed violin, a rehab, played by the leader, a psaltery, and a large assortment of flutes. Gongs and drums provide the punctuating accents. All the instruments play essentially in unison, with each adding their own rhythmic and melodic animations. Even though the pentatonic scale has its limitations, the sound effect is very unique in the world of music.

Because of both the ritualistic and divine origins, the music has little changed since ancient times. Under the constant corrosion of the tropics, wars, migrations, and commercial convulsions, many of the ancient kingdoms have collapsed, but the arts from the past still live on, giving the islanders a common link, especially in Bali, "the world's last paradise," as India's Prime Minister Nehru called it. Of the more than two million Balinese most have some artistic avocation, either in the visual arts or as players in the many gamalan orchestras. They may also dance in fire dances, dagger dances or monkey dances. Most of the dancers respond in hysterical trances, hypnotized by the relentless rhythms of the gamelan. Some even cut themselves during some of their more violent dances, believing that they are warding off the Queen of the Witches' evil magic. Afterwards, their friends treat them by putting red flowers on their wounds.

American Indian Music

Trying to make a generalization of the American Indian is in itself a foolish undertaking. First, we are dealing with minimally 50 languages and the Government Office of Indian Affairs deals at the present with some 302 tribes, not counting many sub-tribal divisions. Each of them have their own religions, culture, customs, and of course their own music.

Nevertheless, most Indian religions and music have a certain communality. Among the Indians, there is a great reverence for nature and a belief in a divine power. Shamans perform sacred rituals and treat the sick and dying with sacred chants. As a matter of fact, songs that belong to a certain custom are only being sung for that purpose. Visitors cannot persuade them to just "demonstrate" that song—for instance, a rain song cannot be performed when that need is not imminent. Music is most often not performed for its own sake, as most music to them has a purpose, a meaning beyond the mere melody or rhythm. They have songs of:

Healing
Medicine
Hunting
Games
Gambling
War
Battle
Victory
Dreams and visions
Children

Love songs

Religious ceremonial songs, etc.

These songs are always sung in unison, and most frequently supported by a larger drum. The rhythms are mostly very irregular and complex, not unlike African polyrhythms, although most often they will use a very simple drum-beating stroke of equal force and timing. Given the fact that the music was transmitted orally it was basically not until the invention of the disk-record (patented in 1896), that serious research could be done, since irregularities of rhythm and pitch defied exact musical notation.

Most of the melodies have a descending motion, which is characteristic of all primitive music and most often the ultimate note is the lowest tone. Many tribes, especially the Patagonian Indians of South America, use mostly only two adjacent notes, while the Hopi Indians, retaining those same notes, have an interesting launching figure into it—also the endings are more elaborate and descent on a different ending note. The medicine-men (shaman) use chant-like incantations, a free recitation with an almost hypnotic effect.

There are a great diversity of instruments, although flutes, whistles, rattles, and drums predominate. Flutes are often used for warnings and whistles are very much part of the shaman's equipment. Rattles are considered sacred and used most often for worship—they are usually receptacles filled with loose objects. Drums are the heart of the Indian music and come in various sizes, ranging from hand drums to large water filled kegs.

One of the first to adapt Indian music into his writings was Dvořák, with his *New World* symphony. Additionally, Busoni used tribal tunes in his Indianisches Tagebuch, as have Edward MacDowell in his *Indian Suite* of 1890 and Victor Herbert in his opera, *Natoma*.

Glossary

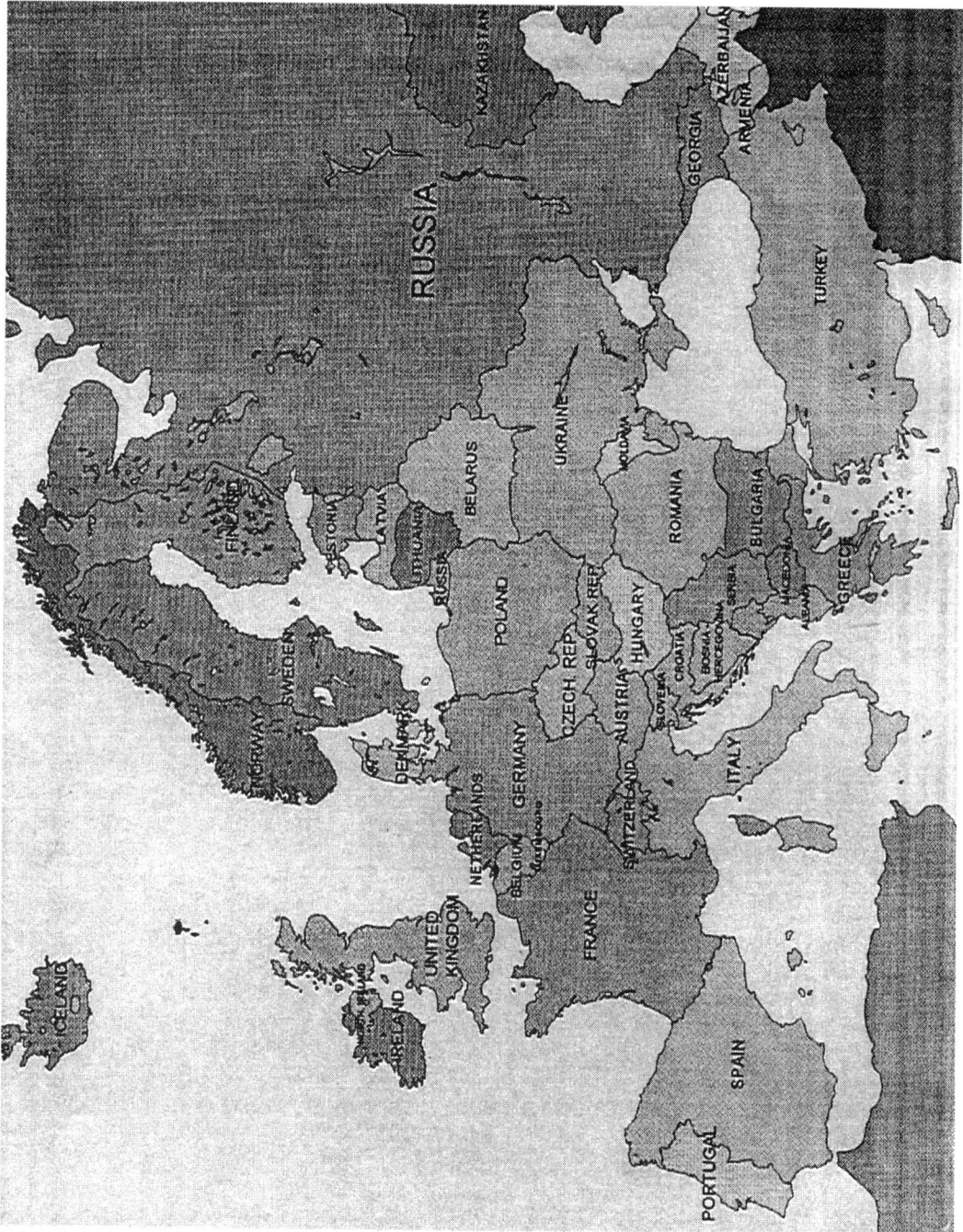

Absolute music:	no extra musical story unlike program music (see)
A cappella:	Choir without instruments
Accellerando:	Gradually faster
Allegro:	Fast, cheerful
Andante:	Walking pace
Aria:	Lyrical song with accompaniment
Atonal:	Has no scale related system
Basso ostinato:	Relentless repeated bass
Binary form:	Two part form AB, usually repeated
Cadence:	Closing effect
Cadenza:	Improvisatory passage in concertos
Chorale:	Lutheran Hymn
Chord:	Three or more tones sounding together (see Consonant & Dissonant)
Coda:	Tailpiece, concluding section
Concerto:	Always implies that one or more instruments are featured.
	(ex. Concerto for violin, Bach)
Concertmaster:	Acts as assistant conductor (see First Chair)
Consonant:	Pleasing chord combination
Contrapunctal:	Same as polyphony, more than one melody combined
Crescendo:	Gradually louder
Development:	In sonata-allegro form, middle section, in which themes are worked out
Decrescendo:	Gradually softer
Dissonant:	Harsh, unpleasant chords
Episode:	Sections between statements especially in fugues and Rondos
Exposition:	Section in which the themes are stated, especially in the Sonata-Allegro Form

Fantasia:	(see Rhapsody)
First chair:	Leader of the different instrumental groups (ex. First Chair of Brass)
Fugue:	Acts like a round, but much more sophisticated. Prominent in the Baroque.
Gregorian chant:	Unison singing as practiced in the Roman Catholic Church. Largely abandoned since 1965.
Harmony:	(see chords)
Homophonic:	Basically a melody accompanied by instruments
Imitation:	Repetition occurring in another voice
Idée fixe:	First used by Berlioz to couple a person or place to a certain melody. Keeps repeating when person is mentioned or appears.
Improvisation:	Create on the spot but, 1. must stay with the prevailing style 2. stay with same tempo 3. stay in same key
Jazz Styles	1. Dixieland 2. Blues 3. Boogie-woogie 4. Swing 5. Big Band 6. Bebop or Bop 7. Progressive 8. Cool, Modem 9. Funky 10. Crossover 11. Fusion
Key:	tonal center, symphonies named after a "key" (scale)
Leitmotiv:	(see Idee fixe)
Linear:	horizontal melodies versus vertical harmony
Lyric:	songlike
Measure:	metric unit in music with a set amount of beats

Major key versus minor key:	major makes generally music happier, minor music is usually serious or sad.
Modulation:	change of key—especially used as of the Baroque period
Motive:	(see theme)
Overture:	originally an opening piece to opera, oratorio, ballet, etc. Eventually an independent piece. Same for Prelude or Toccata.
Plain song:	(see Gregorian chant)
Polyphony:	more than one voice in combination
Program music:	(see Absolute music)
Recitativo:	less elaborate music concentrating on the text, versus Aria

concentrates on the emotion of the moment |
Requiem:	mass for the dead as practiced in the Roman Catholic Church until 1965
Rhapsody:	freely constructed pieces that have no particular form
Ritornello:	short returning passage (see Refrain)
Refrain:	similar to ritornello but much more elaborate
Scale:	stepwise arrangement of notes of a given key
Staccato:	short, detached notes. On violin usually called pizzicato.
Tempo:	rate of speed of music
Suite:	Baroque: a series of dances
Dramatic: independent pieces under one heading; (Nutcracker Suite by Tchaikovsky)
Symphony:	Multi-movement large composition (usually 4 movements)
1. Sonata-Allegro form
2. Three part form, sometimes Theme and Variations
3. Minuet and Trio later as of Beethoven becomes a Scherzo.
4. Rondo or sometime Sonata-Allegro form

Tin-Pan Alley:	a street or district frequented by musicians and composers in the beginning of this century (see Gershwin)
Tone Poem:	large-scale, single movement, programmatic work. (ex. The Sorcerer's Apprentice, Paul Dukas)
Ternary form:	three part form, usually ABA. (ex. Minuet and trio, Minuet)
Score:	each instrument group requires its own line. Used for composing and conducting to oversee all the parts.
Transition:	passage that connects between structural elements of a given form. (ex. Transition between first and second theme in Sonata-Allegro form.)
Vamp:	introductory accompaniment to a song
Virtuoso:	a performer who excels in technical ability

Music Library Centerpieces

That so few like the arts is because
most do not know what life is all about.
—Jean de Boisson

Note: All suggested recordings are on CD's. If no label is mentioned, this is because many good recordings are available. Many clubs have good "deals" on respectable performances with renowned artists and distinguished orchestras.

Medieval

The Benedictine Monks of Santo Domingo de Silos
    Good collection of Gregorian chant

Sequentia (BMG classics)
    Selection of medieval music by Hildegard von Bingen
    Beginnings of polyphony

Renaissance

The Los Angeles Guitar Quartet (Delos DE 3132)
    Dances from the Renaissance to Nutcracker

Masses and Motets by Palestrina
    Especially look for the Papae Marcellus Mass

Peter Warlock: Capriol Suite (excellent)
Allegri: Miserere (Musical Heritage)

Baroque

The Rage of 1710 *(Allegretto)*
    Many familiar pieces by Bach, Handel, Pachelbel, Vivaldi

Top 10 of classical music (Baroque) *(Delta Music)*
    Good selection of the principal composers of the Baroque

Bach, Brandenburg Concertos
    Air from the Suite in D
    Toccata in d

Handel, Messiah (Columbia House)
    Royal Fireworks and Water Music *(Columbia House)*
    The arrival of the Queen of Sheba

Vivaldi, the Four seasons *(Philips)*
    Excellent rendition by the "I Musici"

Pachelbel, Canon in D major

Classical

Haydn, Trumpet Concerto in E-flat *(Columbia House)*
    The London Symphonies

Mozart, Great Composers *(Time-Life Music)*
    Includes: The Marriage of Figaro, Eine kleine Nachtmusik
    Requiem *(Essential Classics—Sony classical)*
    The Great Symphonies *(Delta Music)*
    Concerto for Piano, Concertos for Horn

Beethoven, The Fifth Symphony *(Time-Life Music)*
    Fur Elise
    Sonata for Piano "Pathétique" and "Moonlight"
    Leonore Overture 43, "Egmont" Overture
    The Ninth Symphony, especially the last movement

Romantic

Franz Schubert: Symphony #8, "Unfinished" *(Point Productions)*
    Rosamunde
    The Trout Variations

Berlioz, Symphonie Fantastique *(Columbia House)*
    Requiem
    Roman Carnival
    The Childhood of Christ; The Shepherd's Farewell

Mendelssohn, Violin Concerto in E minor
    Symphony #4 "Italian"
    Fingal's Cave
    Midsummer Night's Dream (Wedding March)

Chopin, Polonaise in A (military)
  Mazurkas
  Fantasie-Impromptu

Bizet, Orchestra] Works, Vol. 11 *(Musical Heritage Society)*
  Carmen Suite
  L'Arlesienne Suite #1

Wagner, Overtures *(Decca-London)*
  Tannhauser
  Meistersinger of Nurnberg
  Tristan and Isolde

Schuman, Piano Concerto, also Poet's love (songs to poems by Heine)

Liszt, Piano Concerto in E-flat *(CBS)*
  Liebestraum
  Les Preludes
  Hungarian Rhapsodies

Mussorgsky, Pictures at an Exhibition *(Deutsche Grammophon)*

Borodin, Polovetsian Dances

Tchaikovsky, Romeo and Juliet *(Time Life)*
  Nutcracker Suite
  Piano Concerto, Capriccio Itallen, Overture "1812" *(Time Life)*

Smetana, From Ma Vlast: The Moldau

Dvorak, Symphony #9 (from the New World)
  Slavonic Dance in g minor

Brahms, Ein Deutsches Requiem
  Symphony #3 and Variations on a Theme by Haydn *(CBS)*

Richard Strauss, Till Eulenspiegel's Merry Pranks *(London)*
  Don Juan

Faure, Requiem

Mahler, Symphony #1 *(Deutsche Grammophon)*
  Songs of a Wayfarer
Sibelius, Finlandia

Rimsky-Korsakov, Scheherazade *(Columbia)*
  Capriccio Espagnol

Grieg, Piano Concerto

Rachmaninov, Rhapsody on a theme by Paganini
   Piano Concerto #2 *(Both on EMI)*

Weber, Invitation to the Dance

Saint-Saens, Danse Macabre
   Carnival of the Animals

Impressionist

Debussy, Prelude to the "Afternoon of a Faun" *(Deutsche Grammophon)*
   La Mer, Images, etc.

Ravel, Bolero, La Valse, Alborado del Gracioso (CBS *Records)*
   Pavane pour une infante defunte

Holst, The Planets

Rodrigo, Concierto de Aranjuez (Guitar concerto)

Respighi, Fountains of Rome, Pines of Rome, Roman Festivals *(London)*

Grofe, Grand Canyon Suite *(BMI)*

De Falla, The Three-cornered Hat *(Columbia)*
   Nights in the Gardens of Spain (Erato)

Dukas, The Sorcerer's Apprentice

Barber, Adagio for Strings

20ᵗʰ Century

Stravinsky, The Rite of Spring
      Petrouchka
      The Firebird
      Symphony of Psalms

Schoenberg, Transfigured Night
      Five pieces for Orchestra

Bartok, Concerto for Orchestra
      Roumanian Dances
      Music for Strings, Percussion and Celeste

Kodaly, Psalmus Hungaricus,
    Hary Janos Suite

Ives, Variations on America
    The Unanswered Question
    Three Places in New England

Gershwin, Rhapsody in Blue
    Variations on "I've got Rhythm"
    American in Paris

Copland, Appalachian Spring
    Hoedown from Rodeo

Bernstein, Overture to Candide
    West Side Story

Prokofiev, "Classical Symphony"
    Peter and the Wolf

Orff, Carmina Burana

Britten, The Young Person's Guide to the Orchestra

Messiaen, Turangalila *(Deutsche Grammophon)*

Milhaud, Le Boeuf sur le Toit
    La création du Monde (the creation of the world)

Shostakovich, Symphony #5 *(Terlarc)*

Hindemith, Mathis der Mahler
    Metamorphis *(London)*

Andrew Lloyd Webber, Requiem, also Cats, Evita, Phantom, etc.

Soundtracks by John Williams

Soundtrack for "Les Miserables"

Corrigliano, Symphony # 1 *(Erato)*

Jazz

Many excellent CD's by Louis Armstrong, Duke Ellington, Glenn Miller, Charlie Parker, Modern Jazz Quartet, Dave Brubeck, John Coltrane, Dizzy Gillespie, Chick Corea and many others.

This is a fairly comprehensive list of works by leading composers. Nevertheless this list really has no end as many valuable works were omitted by necessity. Do not buy everything at once. It takes a lifetime to acquire even a fraction of what is available.

Bibliography and Suggested Readings

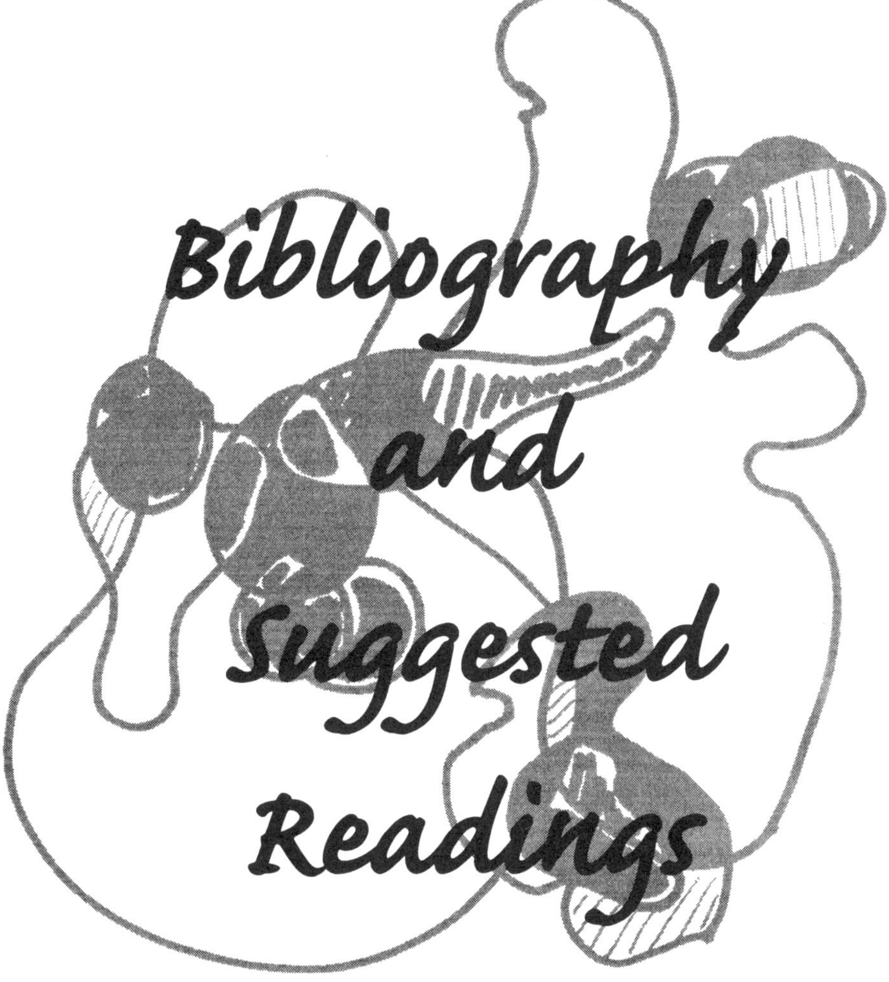

Abraham, Gerald. *The Concise Oxford History of Music.* Oxford, 1979

Ames, V.M., *What is Music?,* journal of Aesthetics and Art Criticism, 1967, 26, 241–249

Apel, Willy. *The Harvard Brief Dictionary of Music.* Cambridge, Harvard University Press, 1970

Austin, William. *Music in the Twentieth Century.* W. W. Norton, 1966

Barr, A., *What is Modern Painting?,* N.Y.: Museum of Modern Art, 1966

Beardsley, M.C., *Aesthetics from Classical Greece to the Present. A Short History,* New York: MacMillan, 1966

Berendt, Joachim, *The Jazz Book-from Ragtime to Fusion,* N.Y.: Lawrence Hill Books, 1989

Bernard, J., *The Music of Edgard Varése,* New Haven: Yale University Press, 1987

Bernstein, L., *The Joy of Music,* N.Y.: Simon & Schuster, 1959

Bernstein, Leonard. *The Joy of Music.* Simon and Schuster Inc., 1965

Bhavnani, E., *The Dance in India: The Origin and History-Classical, Folk and Tribal,* Bombay: D.B. Taraporevala Sons & Co., 1965

Blesh, R. and Janis, H., *They All Played Ragtime.* N.Y.: Oak Publications, 1971

Blume, Friedrich. *Renaissance and Baroque Music.* W. W. Norton, 1967

Boas, F., *Primitive Art,* New York: Dover, 1955

Bowers, Jane and Judith Tick, eds. *Women Making Music.* University of Illinois, 1986

Brooks, Tilford. *America's Black Musical Heritage.* Prentice-Hall, 1984

Bronowski, J. *The Ascent of Man.* Little, Brown and Co., 1973

Brown, H.M., *Music in the Renaissance,* Englewood Cliffs, NJ.: Prentice Hall, 1976

Buber, M., *Images of Good and Evil,* London: Routledge & Kegan Paul, 1952

Bukofzer, Manfred. *Music in the Baroque Era.* Norton, 1967

Burtob, Kim., *World Music,* London: Rough Guides Press, 1994

Buswell, G. T. *How People Look at Pictures.* University of Chicago, 1934

Cage, J., *Silence: Lectures and Writings.* Middletown, Conn.: Wesleyan University Press, 1973

Charters, S., *The Country Blues,* N.Y.: Rinehart, 1959

Cheney, S., *Expressionism in Art,* New York: Tudor, 1948

Chujoy, A. and Manchester, P.W., *Dance Encyclopedia,* New York: Simon & Schuster, 1966

Cope, David. *New Directions in Music. Wm.* C. Brown, 1984

Copland, A., *Music and Imagination,* Cambridge, Mass: Harvard University Press, 1952

Copland, Aaron. *What to Listen for in Music.* New American Library, 1964

Clark, Kenneth. *Civilization.* Harper and Row, Publishers, 1969

Clark, K., *Looking at Pictures,* N.Y.: Rinehart & Winston, 1980

Dan, Nathan, *African-American Music,* N.Y.: Simon & Schuster, 19-

Einstein, Alfred. *Music in the Romantic Era.* W. W. Norton, 1974

Ellington, E.K., *Music is My Mistress,* N.Y.: Doubleday, 1973

Erikson, Rob. *The Structure of Music: A Listener's Guide.* Greenwood Press, 1977

Ewen, David. *The Complete Book of Classical Music* Prentice-Hall N. J., 1965

Freud, S., *Civilisation and Its Discontents,* New York: J. Cope & H. Smith, 1939

Gillespie, D., *George Crumb: A Profile of a Composer.* N.Y.: Peters, 1985

Goldberg, I., *George Gershwin: A Study in American Music,* N.Y.: Simon & Schuster, 1958

Gross, H., *Sound and Form in Modern Poetry: A Study from Thomas Hardy to Robert Lowell,* Ann Arbor: University of Michigan Press, 1964

Grout, D.J., *A History of Western Music,* New York: W.W. Norton & Co., 1960

Grout, D.J., *A Short History of Opera,* N.Y: Columbia Press, 1965

Hanslick, E., *The Beautiful in Music* (1891) reprinted, New York: Liberal Arts Press, 1957

Harris, A.S., *Women Artists 1550-1950,* N.Y.: Knopf, 1977

Hevner, K., *The Affective Value of Pitch and Tempo in Music,* American journal of Psychology, 1937, 49, 621-630

Hiller, L.A., Jr., and Isaacson, L.M., *Experimental Music,* New York: MacGraw-Hill, 1959

Hindemith, P. *A Composer's World: Horizons and Limitations.* Harvard U. Press, 1952

Hitchcock, H., *Music in the United States,* Englewood Cliffs, N.J.: Prentice Hall, 1988

Hoppin, R., *Medieval Music,* N.Y: Norton, 1978

Hunter, S., *Modern French Painting,* New York: Dell, 1956

Jaques-Dalcroze, E., *Rhythm, Music and Education,* New York: Putnam's, 1921

Jones, R., *Music by Philip Glass,* N.Y: Harper & Row, 1987

Kreitler, H. and S. *Psychology of the Arts.* Duke University Press, 1972

Kultermann, U., *The New Sculpture: Environments and Assemblages,* N.Y: Praeger, 1968

Kurth, E., *Musikpsychologie,* Bern: Krumpholz, 1947

Lang, Paul Henry. *Stravinsky, A New Appraisal.* W. W. Norton, 1963

Langfeld, H.S., *The Aesthetic Attitude,* N.Y: Harcourt, Brace, 1920

Lippard, L., Pop *Art,* N.Y: Thames Hudson, 1985

Lowenfeld, V., *The Nature of Creative Activity.* N.Y: Harcourt, Brace, 1939

Macdermott, M. M., *Vowel Sounds in Poetry,* London: Kegan Paul, 1940

Maritain, J., *Creative Intuition in Art and Poetry,* N.Y: Meridian Books, 1955

Mendelowitz, Daniel. *A History of American Art.* Holt, Rinehart and Winston, Inc., 1973

Merleau-Ponty, *Phénoménologie de la perception,* Paris: Gallimard, 1945

Meye; L.B., *Emotion and Meaning in Music,* Chicago: University of Chicago Press, 1956

Morgan, R., *Twentieth-Century Music,* N.Y: Norton, 1991

Moyers, Bill. A *World of Ideas.* Doubleday, 1990

Neuls-Bates, C., *Women in Music: An Anthology of Source Readings from the Middle Ages to the Present,* N.Y: Harper & Row, 1982

Palisca, C., *Baroque Music,* Englewood Cliffs, N.J.: Prentice Hall, 1980

Peelegrini, A., *New Tendencies in Art,* N.Y: Crown, 1966

Piper, J., *Stained Glass: Art or Anti-Art?* N.Y: Reinhold Book Co., 1968

Platinga, L., *Romantic Music,* N.Y: Norton, 1985

Panofsky, E., *Meaning in the Visual Arts,* Garden City, N.Y: Doubleday, 1955

Peyser, J., *Bernstein: A Biography,* N.Y: Morrow, 1987

Ratner, L., *Classic Music: Expression, Form and Style,* N.Y: Schirmer, 1989

Read, H., *The Art of Sculpture,* N.Y: Pantheon Books, 1956

Sessions, R., *The Musical Experience of Composer, Performer, Listener,* Princeton: University Press, 1962

Schrade, L., *Monteverdi, Creator of Modern Music,* N.Y: Norton, 1969

Schuller, G., *The Swing Era: the Development of Jazz 1930-1945,* N.Y: Oxford University Press, 1989

Sowa, J., A *Machine to Compose Music,* N.Y: Oliver Garfield Co., 1956

Stone, E., *The Writings of Elliott Carter,* Bloomington, IN: University of Indiana Press, 1977

Southern, E., *Music of Black Americans*, NX: Norton, 1983

Swain, J., *The Broadway Musical: A Critical and Musical Survey*, N.Y: Oxford University Press, 1990

Taruskin, R., *Essays on Music and Performance*, N.Y: Oxford University Press, 1995

Thurstone, L.L., *The Problem of Melody*, Musical Quarterly, 1920, 6, 426-429

Tirro, E, *jazz, A History*, N.Y: Norton, 1993

Wallis, W.D., *Religion in Primitive Society*, N.Y: Crofts, 1939

Wölfflin, H., *Principles of Art History*, N.Y: Dover Publications, n.d.

Weston, J.L., *From Ritual to Romance*, Garden City, N.Y: Doubleday, 1957

Index

P